Interruptions

Modern and Contemporary Poetics

Interruptions

The Fragmentary Aesthetic in Modern Literature

GERALD L. BRUNS

THE UNIVERSITY OF ALABAMA PRESS

TUSCALOOSA

The University of Alabama Press
Tuscaloosa, Alabama 35487-0380
uapress.ua.edu

Inquiries about reproducing material from this work should
be addressed to the University of Alabama Press.

Typeface: Scala and Eurostile

Cover image: derek beaulieu's poem "Silence (*C'est mon
Dada*)"; courtesy derek beaulieu
Cover design: Michele Myatt Quinn

Library of Congress Cataloging-in-Publication Data

Names: Bruns, Gerald L., author.
Title: Interruptions : the fragmentary aesthetic in modern literature / Gerald L. Bruns.
Description: Tuscaloosa : The University of Alabama Press, [2018] | Series: Modern and
contemporary poetics | Includes bibliographical references and index.
Identifiers: LCCN 2017038241| ISBN 9780817359065 (pbk.) | ISBN 9780817391720 (e book)
Subjects: LCSH: Discourse analysis, Literary. | Literature, Modern—Criticism, Textual. |
Literature, Experimental—Criticism, Textual. | Poetics. | Aesthetics in literature. | Meaning
(Philosophy) in literature. | Intertextuality.
Classification: LCC P302.5 .B78 2018 | DDC 808.001/4—dc23
LC record available at https://lccn.loc.gov/2017038241

For Anne, Eloise, Marga, John, and Jacob

Contents

Preface and Acknowledgments

This book takes its point of departure from a passage in Erich Auerbach's *Mimesis*, where many years ago I first ran across the notion of *parataxis*. It occurs, among other places, in his chapter on *The Song of Roland*, a poem that refuses to follow the traditional logic of sequential narrative: "Instead of a process of complex and periodic development, we have repeated returns to the starting point, each one proceeding to elaborate a different element or motif: in all cases rationally organized condensations are avoided in favor of a halting, spasmodic, juxtapositive, and pro- and retrogressive method in which causal, modal, and even temporal relations are obscured" (2003: 105).

This passage inspired in me a long since lapsed ambition, namely to write a history of fragmentary writing. The present book is something of an effort to pursue that ambition by exploring a variety of examples of self-interrupting composition, starting with some brief pages on Friedrich Schlegel's inaugural theory and practice of the fragment as an assertion of the autonomy of words, their freedom from rule-governed hierarchies. Following Schlegel's idea of a "poetry of poetry"—poetry that is no longer in the service of the church, the state, the school, or any official categories of thought and discourse—the first chapter provides a short history of the fragment as a distinctive feature of literary modernism from Gertrude Stein to Paul Celan and beyond to the present time. The second chapter attends to the later work of Maurice Blanchot and Samuel Beckett and argues that Blanchot's writings on the fragment during the 1950s and early 1960s helped to inspire Beckett's turn toward the paratactic prose of *Comment C'est* (1964) and the even more radical fragmentary fiction of his later years (*Worstward Ho*, for example). Meanwhile, part II of the book studies the radically paratactic arrangements of two contemporary British poets (major figures of the so-called Cambridge school), J. H. Prynne and John Wilkinson, and focuses chiefly on their most recent, and arguably most recondite, works.

A subtext of these proceedings is that any break with what Auerbach calls "classical syntax" (2003: 105) is a break with the whole Western tradition of "apologetics" that, starting with Aristotle and continuing through Wordsworth's preface to the *Lyrical Ballads* and even to this day, attempts to endow poetry with a philosophical seriousness. For example, in one of the first substantial essays on the work of Gertrude Stein, the poet John Ashbery likened her writing to that of the later Henry James. But Stein's innovations are invariably (and inimitably) comic.

Thus chapter 5 may seem at first as a bit of a digression, but in fact, it is itself something of a parody of the "apologetics" tradition, and it opens the way to a close study of the poetry and poetics of Charles Bernstein—paradoxically a poet heavily influenced by the philosopher Stanley Cavell, whose entire work (like Wittgenstein's) is an effort to relocate philosophy at ground level, among the details of everyday life, whose familiarity so often renders us oblivious to the world we in fact inhabit. The hard fact (as Bernstein's poetic career painfully demonstrates) is that this reality is as vulnerable to catastrophe, both public and personal, as it is to the ludic particulars of ordinary experience. Throughout it all, however, Bernstein's ear is tuned to comic one-liners derived from the American idiom that, beginning with William Carlos Williams, so much of American poetry has celebrated.

The final two chapters take up James Joyce—first, the language of *Finnegans Wake*. Whereas up until now parataxis has concerned the breakup of sentences or their juxtaposition as opposed to their "periodic development," here the concern is with the breakup of the word itself, its reassembly into puns, neologisms, nonsense, and even random strings of letters. How to "read," or at all events cope with, such alphabetic play? Critical tradition mainly counsels reading as the repair of Joyce's language, restoring it to plain English. Or, much to the same effect, the practice has been to disregard the linguistic surface in favor of "deep-structure" analyses that claim to lay bare the work's logic of construction. But what if one does not bypass the (invariably comic) experience of the words themselves? Suppose one follows, among other courses, Julia Kristeva's writings on our "erotic" relation to words, or the example of Jacques Derrida's "Wakean" *Glas*? As I have often tried to show over the years, the experience of the materiality of language is one of the principal aesthetic achievements of literary modernism.

The final chapter might seem in this event like a step back from language, but its topic is the paratactic experience of mirrors in Joyce's fiction, particularly in *Dubliners*, the *Portrait*, and *Ulysses*, where mirror experiences are invariably interruptions, discontinuities, or (especially in the "Circe" episode of *Ulysses*) metaphorical displacements and proliferations of self-identity. As the philosopher Emmanuel Levinas says in "Reality and Its Shadow," "a person bears on his face, alongside of its being with which he coincides, its own caricature" (1987: 6). Or, as Stephen Dedalus discovers, our faces seem to multiply as we encounter others during the day (1986: 175). We are not so much ourselves as juxtapositions of alterity. In any event, we seem to have come full circle from the German romantics—for example, Novalis: "The I must be divided into order to be I" (Schulte-Sasse 1997: 102); or again: "The I is only thinkable by means of a *Non-I*; for an I is only an I insofar as it is a Non-I. Otherwise it could be whatever it wanted to be, it just wouldn't be an I" (107).

Je est un autre. (Rimbaud 1962: 6)

The epilogue returns to the writings of Gertrude Stein and her anarchic temporality of "begin again and again" (1972: 305), that is, writing in a "continuous present" (1971: 25) that in principle could go on without end—for example, *The Making of Americans*, a very long book made of sentences with seemingly endlessly deferred periods. Recall Auerbach's description of *The Song of Roland*'s repeated "returns to [its] starting point." Or Blanchot's "infinite conversation." Or the last line of Beckett's *Unnamable*: "I can't go on. I go on." Not to put too fine a point on it: as Philippe Lacoue-Labarthe and Jean-Luc Nancy say, "the fragment involves . . . an essential incompletion" (1988: 42).

I am indebted to a great many people who helped make this book possible—Steve Fredman, Johanna Drucker, Krys Ziarek, Jim Hansen, Julie Carr, and especially Marjorie Perloff, whose writings on literary modernism (from old Vienna to contemporary Brazil) have always been very special to me. I owe a great deal to Jacob Schepers for his help in preparing my manuscript for publication—checking quotations, compiling the works cited, and catching many errors along the way—and to Andy Richardson for his help in producing some high-resolution images for chapter 1. James R. Kincaid meanwhile provided his usual demonic inspiration as I struggled to compose these pages. His laughter has been ringing in my ears now for more than half a century.

The prologue, "The Invention of Poetry," first appeared in *Wordsworth Circle*, 47.2–3 (2016)—part of a Festschrift for Robert Langbaum, who was my mentor and thesis director at the University of Virginia in the early 1960s. Chapter 1, "An Archeology of Fragments," appeared in *Humanities* 3.4 (2016) as part of a special issue edited by Krzysztof Ziarek. Chapter 2, "The Impossible Experience of Words: The Later Fiction of Maurice Blanchot and Samuel Beckett," appeared in *Modern Language Quarterly* 7.2 (2015). Chapter 3, "Dialectrics: Turbulence and Contradiction in J. H. Prynne's *Kazoo Dreamboat*," appeared in the *Chicago Review* 57.3/4 (2013). Chapter 4, "Metastatic Lyricism: John Wilkinson's Poetry and Poetics," appeared in *Textual Practice* 30.4 (2016). Chapter 5, "Apology for Stuffed Owls: On the Virtues of Bad Poetry," appeared in the June 2015 issue of *Volta*. An earlier version of chapter 6, "Paratactics ('Pataquerics') of the Ordinary: The Course of the Comic in Charles Bernstein's Poetry," appeared in *boundary2* 44.4 (2017), copyright © Duke University Press. Chapter 7, "On the Words of the *Wake* (and What to Do with Them)," appeared in *Philological Quarterly* 92.4 (2013). Chapter 8, "What's in a Mirror?: James Joyce's Phenomenology of Misperception," appeared in the *James Joyce Quarterly* 49.3/4 (2013). I am very grateful to these journals for permission to republish this material.

And warm thanks to Charles Bernstein, J. H. Prynne, and John Wilkinson for their permission to cite substantial portions of their work and to John Ashbery for permission to cite two of his poems in chapter 6. "The Problem of Anxiety" was published in his volume *Can You Hear, Bird* (copyright © 1995, 2007, by John Ashbery; all rights reserved). His poem "Laughing Gravy" was published in his volume *Wakefulness* (copyright © 1998, 2007, by John Ashbery; all rights reserved). Both poems were republished in *Notes from the Air; Selected Later Poems* (2007), used by arrangement with Georges Borchardt, Inc., for the author. And special thanks to derek beaulieu for the use of his visual poem from *Silence* (Redfoxx Press, 2010).

This book is for my children and granddaughter.

Interruptions

Prologue

The Invention of Poetry

The romantic kind of poetry is the only one that is more than a kind,
that is, as it were, poetry itself.
—Friedrich Schlegel, "Athenaeum Fragments" #116

Let me begin by exploring some reasons for thinking of the early German romantics—specifically Friedrich Schlegel (1772–1829) and the Athenaeum group (1798–1801)—as the first avant-garde of literary modernism, where poetry is an instance of art *as such*, a form in itself and not (simply) an instrument of mediation in behalf of signification, representation, or expressions of subjectivity.[1] Indeed, the celebrated post-Nietzschean critique of instrumental reason really has its origins in this period (1792–1803). As Friedrich Schlegel's brother, August Wilhelm, responding to Kant's *Critique of Judgment* (1790), argues in his "Theory of Art" (1798), "it is necessary not to treat language in poetry as a mere instrument of the understanding" (Schulte-Sasse 1997: 205; see also Michel and Oksiloff 1997: 157–79).

I. Irony and the Law of Noncontradiction

Of course, the German romantics are perhaps most often remembered for their concept of irony:

> Philosophy is the real homeland of irony, which one would like to define as logical beauty: for whatever appears in oral or written dialogue—and is not simply confined into rigid systems—there irony should be asked for and provided. (Schlegel, *Critical Fragments* #42, 1991: 5)

Note the distinction between dialogue and system. One might say that romantic irony is rooted in the rejection of consecutive reasoning or of any sort of

categorical or systematic thinking—rooted, indeed, in the rejection of the ancient law of noncontradiction, as in Friedrich Schlegel's famous account of Socratic irony:[2]

> Socratic irony is the only involuntary and yet completely deliberate dis-
> simulation. It is equally impossible to feign or divulge it. . . . In this sort of
> irony, everything originates in the union of *savoir faire* and scientific spirit,
> in the conjunction of a perfectly instinctive and a perfectly conscious phi-
> losophy. It contains and arouses a feeling of indissoluble antagonism be-
> tween the absolute and the relative, between the impossibility and the ne-
> cessity of complete communication. It is the freest of all licenses, for by
> its means one transcends oneself; and yet it is also the most lawful, for it
> is absolutely necessary. It is a very good sign when the harmonious bores
> are at a loss about how they should react to this continuous self-parody,
> when they fluctuate endlessly between belief and disbelief until they get
> dizzy and take what is meant as a joke seriously and what is meant seri-
> ously as a joke.[3] (*Critical Fragments* #108, 1991: 13)

In short, irony is philosophically opposed to Hegelian thinking: irony is not dialectical (the construction of hierarchies) but paradoxical—"Irony is the form of
paradox. Paradox is everything simultaneously good and great" (*Critical Fragments* #48, 1991: 6)—which is no doubt why Hegel turned against the romantics.[4] Irony does not subsume the many into one but instead arranges them as
singularities in a series, whence dialogue displaces dialectic, where "dialogue is
a chain or garland of fragments" (*Athenaeum Fragments* #77, 1991: 27), or what
we modernists would now call "open form" (Hejinian 2001: esp. 43). Schlegel
again:

> An idea is a concept perfected to the point of irony, an absolute synthesis
> of absolute antitheses, the continual self-creating interchange of two con-
> flicting thoughts. (*Athenaeum Fragments* #121, 1991: 33)

As if "absolute synthesis" were not the integration of opposites into a higher
order but a dialogical project ("continual self-creating interchange"), whose goal
is to defer resolution or agreement indefinitely, as in Maurice Blanchot's "infinite conversation."[5] To be a romantic is to be, not of one mind, but always
of another. ("The I must be divided into order to be I," writes Novalis in his
"Fichte Studies" [1795–96].)[6] In any case, the "I" remains open, unfinished (like
the conversation, an unmanaged meeting of minds that do not merge): "Even

a friendly conversation which cannot be freely broken off at any moment, completely arbitrarily, has something intolerant about it" (Schlegel, *Critical Fragments* #37, 1991: 5).

Hence Friedrich Schlegel's polemical fragments against logic, which is always in search of conclusions that hang neatly together:

> Formal logic and empirical psychology are philosophical grotesques. (*Atheneum Fragments* #75, 1991: 27)

> Logic is neither the preface, nor the instrument, nor the formula, nor the episode of philosophy. It is, rather, a coordinated pragmatic science opposed to poetry and to ethics and deriving from the demand for a positive truth and the premise of the possibility of a system. (*Atheneum Fragments* #91, 1991: 29)

> The critics are always talking about *rules*, but where are the rules that are really poetic and applicable for all works of art and not merely grammatical, metrical, logical? (Schulte-Sasse "Fragments on Literature and Poesy" #286, 1997: 332)

Poetry, in short, is not a rule-governed activity: "Poetry is republican speech: a speech which is its own law and an end unto itself, and in which all the parts are free citizens and have the right to vote" (*Critical Fragments* #65, 1991: 8).

II. On Poetry as Such

Friedrich Schlegel's canonical statement of romantic poetics reads in part as follows:

> The romantic kind of poetry is still in the state of becoming; that, in fact, is its real essence; that it should forever be becoming and never be perfected. It can be exhausted by no theory and only a divinatory criticism would dare try to characterize its ideal. It alone is infinite, just as it alone is free; and it recognizes as its first commandment that the will of the poet can tolerate no law above itself. The romantic kind of poetry is the only one that is more than a kind, that is, as it were, poetry itself; for in a certain sense all poetry is or should be romantic.[7] (*Athenaeum Fragments* #116, 1991: 32)

One might be tempted to describe this as something like an anarchic theory of poetry—and, on a certain view, it is: poetry has a history rather than an essence and so resists definitions, concepts, theories, or the status of an ideal. Poetry is local and contingent: "A definition of poetry can only determine what poetry should be, not what it really was and is; otherwise the shortest definition would be that poetry is whatever has at any time and place been called poetry" (*Athenaeum Fragments* #114, 1991: 31).

However, this does not mean that the romantics are not comprehensive in their thinking. What is perhaps most striking is that they are classicists who, among other things, emancipated poetry from the classical (rhetorical) system of genres.[8] Friedrich Schlegel expresses the matter quite bluntly. "All the classical poetical genres have now become ridiculous in their purity" (*Critical Fragments* #60, 1991: 8). And again:

> Should poetry simply be divided up? Or should it remain one and indivisible? Or fluctuate between division and union? Most of the ways of conceiving a poetical world are still as primitive and childish as the old pre-Copernican ideas of astronomy. The usual classifications of poetry are mere dead pedantry designed for people with limited vision. (*Athenaeum Fragments* #434, 1991: 90)

Not that Schlegel's thinking proceeds without contradicting itself—it would, paradoxically, be self-contradictory if it did. For example: "The frequent neglect of the subcategories of genres is a great detriment to a theory of poetical forms" (*Athenaeum Fragments* #4, 1991: 18). But his idea seems to be that poetry is a nonexclusionary form or what he at one point refers to as "transcendental poetry":

> There is a kind of poetry whose essence lies in the relation between ideal and real, and which therefore, by analogy to philosophical jargon, should be called transcendental poetry. It begins in satire in the absolute difference between ideal and real, hovers in between as elegy, and ends as idyll with the absolute identity of the two. . . . [This] sort of poetry should unite the transcendental raw materials and preliminaries of a theory of poetic creativity—often met with in modern poets—with the artistic reflection and beautiful self-mirroring that is present in Pindar, in the lyric fragments of the Greeks, in the classical elegy, and, among the moderns, in Goethe. In all its descriptions, this poetry should describe itself, and always be simultaneously poetry and the poetry of poetry. (*Athenaeum Fragments* #238, 1991: 50)

A "poetry of poetry" would be a form that absorbs (and neutralizes) all distinctions—among them the distinction between verse and prose, which perhaps helps to explain why the romantics proposed that loose and baggy monster, the novel, as the form that most fully embodies their conception of poetry:[9]

> The opinion that the *novel* is not a poem is based on the proposition *All poetry should be metrical*. But for the purpose of furthering progressivity and for this purpose alone, an exception can be made to this proposition. The novel is a yet incomparably more mixed *poetic mélange* than the idyll or satire, which do follow a specific law of *mixture*. (Schulte-Sasse, "Fragments on Literature and Poesy" #4, 1997: 329; Behler 1978)

In "Letter on the Novel," Friedrich Schlegel says that "our poetic art began and ended with the novel [*Roman*]"—so long as it is understood that the novel is not, among other kinds of writing, (simply) a species of narrative. "I . . . loathe the novel," Schlegel says, "insofar as it is a particular genre" (Schulte-Sasse 1997: 193). As examples of the novel, Schlegel mentions Boccaccio, Shakespeare, and Cervantes, whose writings are nothing if not formal *mixtures*. Schlegel puts it, again, bluntly: "I can hardly conceive of the novel as anything but a mixture of narrative, song, and other forms" (193). (Schlegel would certainly have admired Jorge Luis Borges's Library of Babel, which contains somewhere on its indefinite number of shelves a text that contains the very words you are reading now).

Here, were there world enough and time, would be the place to examine Friedrich Schlegel's novel, *Lucinde* (1799), whose (basically) plotless narrative is made of reflections, confessions, idylls, essays, letters, and a dialogue.[10] *Lucinde* is very much in the tradition of Rabelais's *Gargantua and Pantagruel*, with its pages of lists, Laurence Sterne's *The Life and Opinions of Tristram Shandy*—a novel of digressions—and modern experimental novels like Gilbert Sorrentino's *Mulligan Stew* (1979), a collection of heterogeneous documents—letters, lists, notebooks, journal entries, essays, scrapbook items, songs and poems, and a dramatic work, "Flawless Play Restored: A Masque of Fungo"—the whole describing the decline and fall of Anthony Lamont, a writer of bad fiction (Bruns 1981).

III. Form and Fragment

In a 1920 essay on the German romantics, Walter Benjamin writes: "The Romantic theory of the artwork is the theory of its form" (1996: 155). Furthermore: "Every form as such counts as a peculiar modification of the self-limitation of reflection, because it is not a means to the representation of a content" (1996: 158). Paradoxically, the form of the artwork (the poem) is both *pure*—no longer a function of its contents—and yet at the same time a *complexity*. Imagine, as chaos theorists do, something like a turbulence of forms. As Friedrich Schlegel writes:

> The romantic form is *prosaic epos*. (Schulte-Sasse, "Fragments on Literature and Poesy" #394, 1997: 333)
>
> The Romantic imperative demands the mixing of all poetic genres. (Schulte-Sasse, "Fragments on Literature and Poesy" #586, 1997: 334)

In any event, the artwork is very far from being Aristotelian, that is, a construction of parts cohering into a unity that invites admiration. As Benjamin says:

> Form is no longer the expression of beauty but an expression of the idea of art itself. In the final analysis, the concept of beauty has to retreat from the Romantic philosophy of art altogether, not only because, in the rationalist conception, this concept is implicated with that of rules, but above all because as an object of "delight," of pleasure, of taste, beauty seemed incompatible with the austere sobriety that, according to the new conception, defines the essence of art. (1996: 176–77)

The notion of "austere sobriety" is worth some attention. It suggests that the romantic artwork is constructive rather than expressive—for, indeed, the artist is no longer an "I" but (anticipating Flaubert, Mallarmé, Joyce, et al.) an absence—indifferent, paring fingernails: "In order to write well about something, one shouldn't be interested in it any longer. To express an idea with due circumspection, one must have relegated it wholly to one's past. As long as the artist is in the heat of discovery and inspiration, he is in a state which, as far as communication is concerned, is at the very least intolerant" (Schlegel, *Critical Fragments* #37, 1991: 4).

So much, one might say, for Wordsworth's "spontaneous overflow of powerful feelings" (1965: 448)—although it is important to remember that Wordsworth, like the German romantics, distinguished poetry, not from prose but from the logical procedures of "Matter of Fact, or Science" (1965: 451).

Feeling, in any event, is here a feeling for form, as when Friedrich Schlegel speaks, for example, of a "feeling for fragments" (*Athenaeum Fragments* #22,

1991: 21), which, among other things, allows one to think serially, or maybe one should say *ironically*, free of the law of noncontradiction or of any principle of subordination. Or imagine space free of time:

> Fragmentation, the mark of a coherence all the firmer in that it has to come undone in order to be reached, and reached not through a dispersed system, or through dispersion as a system, for fragmentation is the pulling to pieces (the tearing) of that which never has preexisted (really or ideally) as a whole, nor can it ever be reassembled in any future presence whatever. Fragmentation is the spacing, the separation effected by a temporalization which can only be understood—fallaciously—as the absence of time. (Blanchot 1986: 60)

And so one is free, like Wittgenstein, from beginnings, middles, and ends (free, in other words, to stop).

PART I

1

An Archeology of Fragments

A new kind of arrangement not entailing harmony, concordance, or
reconciliation, but that accepts disjunction or divergence as the infinite
center from out of which, through speech, relation is to be created: an
arrangement that does not compose but juxtaposes, that is to say, leaves
each of the terms that come into relation outside one another, respecting
and preserving this exteriority *and this* distance *as the principle—*
always already undercut [toujours déjà destitué]—of all signification.
Juxtaposition and interruption here assume [de chargent ici] an
extraordinary force of justice.
—Maurice Blanchot, "The Fragment Word"

I

It is always prudent to begin with a distinction.

On the one hand, there are ruins, citations, aphorisms, epigrams, paradoxes, remarks (*Bemerkungen*), notes, lists, sketches, marginalia, parentheticals, conversations, dangling participles. . . .

On the other, there is the *objectivist* tradition of romantic poetics that comes down to us from (among others) Friedrich Schlegel, for whom writing is less the work of an expressive subject than an arrangement of words that cannot be contained within any genre description, or indeed within any binary relation, whether between subject and object, part and whole, identity and difference, digit and system, beginning and end.[1]

From Friedrich Schlegel's "Atheneum Fragments" (1798):

> Fr. 24. Many of the works of ancients have become fragments. Many modern works [*der Neuern*] are fragments as soon as they are written.

> Fr. 40. Notes to a poem are like anatomical lectures on a piece of roast beef.

Fr. 46. According to the way many philosophers think, a regiment of soldiers on parade is a system.

Fr. 75. Formal logic and empirical psychology have become philosophical grotesques. (1991: 21, 23, 27, 2013: 23, 25, 29)

Recall Schlegel's characterization of romantic poetry as essentially unfinished —"forever becoming [*ewig nur werden*] and never perfected" (1991: 32, 2013: 34). Or, much to the same point, his disappointment "in not finding in Kant's family tree of basic concepts the category of 'almost' [*die Kategorie Beinahe*], a category that has surely accomplished, and spoiled, as much in the world and in literature as in any other" (1991: 10, 2013: 13).

Incompletion.

Maurice Blanchot: "Let there be a past, let there be a future, with nothing that would allow the passage from one to the other, such that the line of demarcation would unmark them, the more it remained invisible" (1992: 12, 1973: 22).

Gertrude Stein: "The composition forming around me was a prolonged present" (1971: 25).

Almost: no longer, not yet: the *entretemps*—*meanwhile* or *between*—that leaves everything open, as in the white space of a page that interrupts the consecutiveness of such things as sentences, propositions, judgments, arguments, narratives . . . .

Reasoning (putting things together, adding them up): its adversary has always been the anomaly . . . the random particle . . . the missing piece. . . .

To be sure, Schlegel's "fragments" are fairly traditional insofar as they are, like aphorisms, fully integrated predications:

A fragment, like a miniature work of art, has to be entirely isolated [*abgesondert*] from the surrounding world and be complete in itself like a porcupine [*Igel*].[2] (1991: 45, 2013: 48)

Or, like *pensées*, they sometimes extend for several periods, as does his famous fragment on Socratic irony, with its cheerful defiance of the law of noncontradiction:

In this sort of irony, everything should be playful and serious, guilelessly open and deeply hidden. It originates in the union of *savoir vivre* and scientific spirit, in the conjunction of a perfectly instinctive and perfectly conscious philosophy. It contains and arouses a feeling of indissoluble antagonism between the absolute and the relative, between the impossibility and the necessity of complete communication.[3]

Defiance of laws is perhaps a condition of fragmentary writing. But the chief point is that a fragment, whatever its internal arrangement, is not part of any hermeneutical circle, which is, after all, made of links rather than breaks. Think of it (the fragment) as a freak or vagrant, or as part of an amorphous collection of pieces that are not attached to one another (as in a Riemann space).[4]

Elias Canetti: "Keep things apart, keep sentences separate [*die Sätze auseinanderhalten*], or else they turn into colors" (1994: 151).

II

To put it in a slightly different way, on Schlegel's theory a romantic poem would be fragmentary on its own terms, as if from the inside out, as in one of the unpublished works of Friedrich Hölderlin (1770–1843):

Zu Sokrates Zeiten

Vormals richtete Gott.

Könige.

Weise.

wer richtet den izt?

Richtet das einige

Volk? Die heilge Gemeinde?

Nein! o nein! wer richtet denn itzt?

ein Natterngeschlecht!   feig und falsch

das edlere Wort nicht mehr

Über die Lippe

O im Nahmen

ruf ich,

Alter Dämon! dich herab

Oder   sende

Einen Helden

Oder
    die Weisheit.[5] (1969: 241–42)

With Hölderlin, such a random distribution of words across the white space of the page is called "madness"; by the end of the century, with Mallarmé's *Un coup de dès*, it is called "art" (see Sewell 1952 and 1985: 49–69).

Theodor Adorno (1992: 130): "Great music is aconceptual synthesis; this is the prototype for Hölderlin's late poetry, just as Hölderlin's idea of song [*Gesang*] holds strictly for music: an abandoned, flowing nature that transcends itself precisely through having escaped from the spell of the domination of nature [that is, rationality, whose task is to bring everything under control: to put everything in order—and keep it there]."

Following Adorno, one could think of the fragment (as indeed Maurice Blanchot thinks of it) as the achievement of an aesthetics of freedom (Bruns 1997: 89–101).

Even more than Schlegel's, Hölderlin's writing is refractory to any consecutive logic that seeks to reduce the singularity of things to totalities of various kinds. In Adorno's words, like serial music, "it becomes a constitutive dissociation" (1992: 130).

Just so, "dissolution" (die Auflösen) is arguably the watchword of Hölderlin's thinking, as in his essay "Das Werden im Vergehen" (Becoming in Dissolution)," where *Auflösen* is something like a condition of possibility for both art and life, as well as the distinctive feature of Hölderlin's prose (resist now, if you can, the practice of skimming or skipping a long citation):

The new life, which had to **dissolve** [*das sich auflösen solltes*] and did **dissolve**, is now truly possible (of ideal age); **dissolution** is necessary [*die Auflösung notwendig*] and holds its peculiar character between being and non-being. In the state between being and non-being, however, the possible becomes real everywhere, and the real becomes ideal, and in the free imitation of art [*der freien Kunstnachahmung*] this is a frightful yet divine dream. In the perspective of ideal recollection, then, **dissolution** as a necessity becomes as such the ideal object of the newly developed life, a glance back on the path that had to be taken, from the beginning of **dissolution** up to that moment when, in the new life, there can occur a recollection of the **dissolved** and thus, as explanation and union of the gap and the contrast occurring between past and present, there can occur the recollection of **dissolution**. This idealistic **dissolution** is fearless. The beginning and endpoint is already posited, found, secured; and hence this **dissolution** is also more secure, more relentless, more bold [*gesetzt, gefunden, gesichert*], and as such it therefore presents itself as a reproductive act by means of which life runs through all its moments and, in order to achieve the total sum, stays at none but **dissolves** in everyone so as to constitute itself in the next; except that the **dissolution** becomes more ideal to the extent that it moves away from the beginning point, whereas the production becomes more real to the extent that finally, out of the sum of these sentiments of decline and becoming which are infinitely experienced in one moment, there emerges by way of recollection (due to the necessity of the object in the most finite state) a complete sentiment of existence, the initially **dissolved** [*das anfänglich aufgelöste*]; and after this recollection of the **dissolved**, individual matter has been united with the infinite sentiment of existence through the recollecting of the **dissolution**, and after the gap between the aforesaid has been closed, there emerges from this union and adequation of the particular of the past and the infinite of the present the actual new state, the next step that shall follow the past one.[6] (2009: 97–98, 642–43; bold added)

In other words, dissolution is life's mode of existence, but it is not a negative condition; rather, it is "a reproductive act" that generates the temporality "between
being and non-being" (. . . *becoming* . . .); or, much to the same point, it is an always less than final cause that keeps things from standing still, settling down,
or closing up—a protean metaphysics with which Hölderlin's writing achieves
a nearly perfect decorum: dissolution as the principle of *open form*. Think of
Hölderlin, and perhaps the German romantics more generally, as pretheorists
of *complexity*—that is, chaos, turbulence, and Brownian motion (Gleick 1987:
121–25; Waldrop 1992).

In any event, Hölderlin's writing, whether verse or prose, is structured like
the weather.

III

As is Mallarmé's *Un coup de dés* (1992: 430–31):

> *Une insinuation*   *simple*
>   *au silence*   *enroulée avec ironie*
>
>   *ou*
>
>   *le mystère*
>   *récipité*
>   *hurlé*
>
> *dans quelque proche*   *tourbillon d'hilarité et d'horreur*
>   *voltage*   *autour du gouffe*
>
>   *ans le joucher*
>   *ni fuir*
>   *et en berce le vierge indice.*[7]

One has to love the line "tourbillon d'hilarité et d'horreur" (turbulence of
hilarity and horror). Of course, Mallarmé thought of his poem as symphonic
rather than meteorological, but as Adorno suggested with respect to Hölderlin's
fragment, complexity (not harmony) is what gives music and poetry, different
as they are, their family resemblance ("modernism"). Here one should consult
Kate van Orden's study, "On the Side of Poetry and Chaos: Mallarméan *Hasard*
and Twentieth-Century Music" (Temple 1998: 173)—

Much of the "musicality" of Mallarmé's verse arises from its refusal of the
linear and narrative, just as its most radical implications—the coexistence

of chance and art—depend on its adoption of open, recursive, and even potentially chaotic structures.

—which takes up Mallarmé's influence upon Pierre Boulez, Marcel Duchamp, and especially John Cage, whose "Empty Words" is a text in which, as in *Un coup de dés*, typography replaces syntax (and, further, upends the subordination of letters to words):

notAt evening	bon pitch to a truer wordgenerality the
right can see	shoal and weed places
suited to the morning hour	by her perseverancekind veiled
	no longer absorbed ten
	succeededbetween the last hoeing
trucksrsq Measured tSee t A	and the digging the mice many
ys sfOi w dee e str cais	of swampsaio against its white body
	lastno less than partridges
stkva o dcommoncurious 20	ncthe e or day of the sun.

(Cage 1981: 12)

In the preface to "Empty Words" (1981: 11) Cage writes:

> *Syntax*: arrangement of the army (*Norman Brown*). *Language free of syntax: demilitarization of language. James Joyce = new words: old syntax. Ancient Chinese:* Full words: words free of specific function. Noun is verbs is adjective, adverb. *What can be done with the English language? Use it as material. Material of five kinds: letters, syllables, words, phrases, sentences. A text for a song can be a vocalise: just letters.*

IV

Language free of syntax. (Spellcheck: "Fragment. Consider revising.")

Adorno (1997: 147): "Art that makes the highest claim compels itself beyond form as totality and into the fragmentary."

Cage was among the earliest of Gertrude Stein's champions. I think of Stein (along with Hölderlin and Mallarmé) as the first modernist—the one for whom *parataxis* became a regulating principle of poetics. The *locus classicus* is *Tender Buttons* (1914):

IN BETWEEN

In between a place and candy is a narrow foot-path that shows more mount-
ing than anything, so much really that a calling meaning a bolster mea-
sured a whole thing with that. A virgin a whole virgin is judged made and
so between curves and outlines and real seasons and more out glasses and
a perfectly unprecedented arrangement between old ladies and mild colds
there is no satin wood shining. (Stein 2002: 24; Schuster 2011)

A "perfectly unprecedented arrangement between old ladies and mild colds" is
certainly conceivable, but concepts and possibilities require contexts, and contexts depend upon syntax (*s* is *p*). Otherwise there is no "aboutness," as philosophers say.[8] Just so, *parataxis* foregrounds the "between": the break, pause,
swerve, or stammer that materializes the word in a space (or interminability)
of its own.[9]

Naturally thoughts fly to Stein's "Arthur: A Grammar" (1931)—again, avoid
the impulse to skip or skim and ask: How is reading to cope with an arrangement like the following that does not compose but juxtaposes?

Raise which does demean apply in disposition fanned in entirely that
a pre-appointment makes nack arouse preventable security of in approach
call penalty by ingrain fasten copy for the considerable within usual declaration with vicissitude plainly coupled of announcement they can pry
with a coupled for the attachment in a peculiar disturb in a checking of a
particular remained that they fairly come with a calling around for land
shatter just a point with all might in fairly distaste just with a bettering
of likely as well in effect to be doubtfully remark what is a tomato to the
capture do be blindly in ignominy pertain fasten finally in cohesion comply their gross of a tendency polite in recourse of the clambering deny for
like in the complying of a jeopardy so soon does interrelate the way meant
comply in this not a day called restively complaisant definite just whether
it is melodious for the shut of practice that is made with apply clear have
it is a couple of their having it make leave about so much better after a
minute. It is not of any importance that they like to be very well. A grammar means positively no prayer for a decline of pressure. (Stein 1975:
39–40)

Interesting the way terms of connection abound in this passage: "fasten," "couple,"
"attachment," "capture," "cohesion," "interrelate." But for all of that it remains a

"declaration with vicissitude." And whatever one makes of it ("whether it is melodious"), one can still hear Stein's distinctive whimsy: " . . . what is a tomato."

Among other things, as Stein understood, parataxis entails the obsolescence of the comma ("I have refused them so often and left them out so much and did without them so continually that I have come finally to be indifferent to them").[10] The comma, after all, is a structuring device (a "traffic signal," in Adorno's metaphor [1990: 303])—but where, in the long paragraph above, would you place a comma without being merely arbitrary, since it is, until the very end, a paragraph without a sentence (and therefore not a paragraph, but a fragment).

> What is a sentence. One in one. One an one. A sentence is a disappointment. (Stein, "Sentences," 1975: 158)

By contrast:

> Made at random.
> Is random a noun. It is not. It is a pleasure because with because which
> is an allowance with their and on account. (Stein, "Sentences," 1975: 188)

Sentences and, indeed, regularities of every kind are disappointing because they are predictable (understanding is predicated upon the resolution of expectations). Whereas "random" is not a noun or adjective or any part of speech but only a word, that is, a pleasure because it is free, a term liberated from the logical and cognitive regimens that normally rule its (your) life. As William Carlos Williams said of Stein in 1930: "The feeling is of words themselves, a curious immediate quality quite apart from their meaning, much as in music, different notes are dropped, so to speak, into a repeated chord one at a time, one after another—for itself alone" (1970: 347).[11]

But what is a word when it is just itself? Or, as Johanna Drucker asks (2013b: 33–45): "What is a Word's Body?"

V

Imagine a text made of adverbs. Or—

Elias Canetti: "A thinker of prepositions" (1994: 193).

Totalities—propositions, arguments, narratives, treatises, systems—are serious, and therefore philosophical. By contrast, breaks in a pattern—let me call them "singularities"—are comic:

A LITTLE CALLED PAULINE

> A little called anything shows shudders.
> Come and say what prints all day. A whole few
> watermelon.   There is no pope.
> No cut in pennies and little dressing and choose
> wide soles and little spats really little spices. (Stein 2002: 25)

The inclination of critics, as a way of rescuing Stein from decades of ridicule, has been to emphasize her seriousness. John Ashbery, for example, in a review of *Stanzas in Meditation* (1932), likened her poem to Henry James's *The Golden Bowl* (Ashbery 1957: 250). To be sure, the "voice" of *Stanzas* seems at first very different from that of *Tender Buttons*—neutral, distanced, abstract. Ashbery notes that "these austere 'stanzas' are made up almost entirely of colorless connecting words such as 'where,' 'which,' 'these,' 'of,' 'not,' 'have,' 'about,' and so on. . . . The result is like certain monochrome de Kooning paintings in which isolated strokes of color take on a deliciousness they never could have had out of context, or a piece of music by Webern in which a single note on the celesta suddenly irrigates a whole desert of dry, scratchy sounds in the strings" (1957: 250).

A monochrome with certain strokes of color—for example, in Stein's *Stanzas in Meditation*:

> I think well of meaning. (1994: 35)
> More than they wish it is often that it is a disappointment
> To find white turkeys. . . . (52)
> I have lost the thread of my discourse. (155)
> I am trying to say something but I have not said it.
> Why.
> Because I add my I. (183)
> Thank you for hurrying through. (217)

But it remains true that *Tender Buttons*, with its ludic juxtapositions, is one of the great comic poems in English:

> A ham is proud of cocoanut. (49)
> Startling a starving husband is certainly not disagreeable. (66)
> The best game is that which is shiny and scratching. (77)

One could pursue these matters by taking note of the "worsening words" of Samuel Beckett's later paratactic writings, as in *Worstward Ho* (1996: 104):

> What when words gone? None for what then. But say by way of somehow on somehow with sight to do. With less of sight. Still dim and yet—. No. Nohow so on. Say better worse words gone when nohow on. Still dim and nohow on. All seen and nohow on. What words for what then? None for what then. No words for what when words gone. For what when nohow on. Somehow nohow on.

Or Joan Retallack's "ditto Marcel Duchamp? ditto Gertrude Stein?" (1998: 107):

> º. gravel sounds path . eix- . 4 imported . in ver ted yel low
> syn tax . use yellow sponge . thought movie . free taboo
> variant . I don't think we've . leip- . blue caught between
> . angp arek- . el Popo . look in mirror Elaine looking at .
> i-   pronominal stem . meaning of "quickness" . change
> your body? . developing and abandoning vocabularies .

VI

The critic Hugh Kenner (1987: 37–60) associated the advent of modernism with the invention of the typewriter, which (as in the layout of Ezra Pound's pages in the *Cantos*) is able to give the white space of the page a third dimension that words and letters *inhabit* rather than simply a surface that their accumulations obscure.[12] And few understood the comic potential of this transformation of the page as well as did e. e. cummings (1998: 18; Rothenberg 1974: 16):

> NO THANKS. NO. 13
> 　　　　　　r-p-p-h-e-s-s-a-g-r
> 　　　　who
>
> a) s w (e loo) k
> upnowgath
> 　　　　PPEGORHRASS
> 　　　　　　eringint (o-
> a The) : l

                                eA
                          !p:
         S   a

                                      (r
         rIvInG   -gRrEaPsPhOs)
         rea (be) rran (com) gi (e) ngly
         ,grasshopper;

In an essay on "The Open Work of Art" (1955), the Brazilian poet Haroldo de
Campos (2007: 221–22) writes: "For Cummings, the word is fissile [divisible].
His poems have as their fundamental element the 'letter.' The syllable is, for
his needs, already a complex material. The 'tactile modesty' of that poetic attitude is similar to that of Webern: interested in the word on the phonemic level,
he orients himself toward an open poetic form, in spite of the danger of ex-
hausting himself in the one minute poem, as he faces the hindrances of a still
experimental syntax."

   Of course, "NO THANKS. NO. 13" is "language free of syntax."

   As is, for comparison, Charles Bernstein's "Azoot D'Pound" (2000: 161):

   iz wurry ra aZoOt de puund in reducey ap crrRisLe ehk
   nugkinj sJuxYY senshl. ig si heh hahpae uvd r fahbeh aht si
   gidrid. impOg qwbk tug. jr'ghtpihqw. ray aGh nunCe ip
   gvvn EapdEh a' gum riff a' eppehone. ig ew oplep lucd nvn
   atik o. im. ellek Emb ith ott enghip ag ossp heh ooz. ig.

How should one read such a poem? On this question it is useful to follow
Walter Benjamin's "Program for Literary Criticism" (1930): "Good criticism is
composed of at most two elements: the critical gloss and the quotation. Very
good criticism can be made of both glosses and quotations. What must be
avoided like the plague is rehearsing the summary of the contents. In contrast,
a criticism consisting entirely of quotations should be developed" (1999: 290).

   A typewriter poem like Bernstein's offers little to gloss—indeed, as semantic
arrangements, typographic constructions of various kinds (via letterpress, for
example) are seldom interesting—whence the best recourse is the excavation
of historical contexts of the kind that Johanna Drucker provides in *The Visible
Word: Experimental Typography and Modern Art, 1909–23* (1994: 168–92), which
examines crucial avant-garde texts from Marinetti, Apollinaire, and especially
Ilia Zdanevich, a.k.a. Iliazd (1894–1975):[13]

жапиндрОн
ипърижапиндрО **Н**
исвятЫй запъридУхяй
вакрУ гдОхлай
    абУдучи hдОндиж
ТишыНА

Ы

запъридУхяй

лvбvтV гvспV хvсv ‖V
мхvмтV рvчiкV плvмлvвлvклvччьлvблV
сVрпvпv бVчiмv
хтvпvлтV ткvлтvтV тvпvтV
цхvнvжрVхv мтvтV
фvздvбVтvтvтv

Ш

Ю

чiдVчi фvфvсхV
нiпхvмvнiбvсхV
рvвV сv НvКv
пvчiвV чiвV
чiчiгV
бvбvндvбV
хvзнvрvфvсцV

vхvхV цvвvсхV

С В V

скV ргV пнV

мъчьхV лшV кvтvфV
бдV бvгбvлдV

хазЯни

ВаIМ я бОга аслА

Iliazd is one of the inspirations of the "typewriter poetry" that flourished during the 1960s (and beyond)—for example, Alan Riddell's "hologrammer" (Finch 1972: 19):

```
           o              n              a
          pos            ons            fan
          xposu          const          ofani
          exposur        econsti        nofanim
          eexposure      reconstit      onofanima
         heexposurea dreconstitu onofanimag
        theexposureandreconstitutionofanimage
         heexposurea dreconstitu ionofanimag
          eexposure      reconstit      onofanima
          exposur        econsti        nofani
          xposu          const          ofani
          pos            ons            fan
           o              n              a
          p s            o s            f n
         x   u          c   t          o   i
        e     r        e     i        n     m
       e       e      r       t      o       a
      h         a    d         u    i         g
     t           n            t               e
      h         a    d         u    i         g
       e       e      r       t      o       a
        e     r        e     i        n     m
         x   u          c   t          o   i
          p s            o s            f n
           o              n              a
          pos            ons            fan
          xposu          const          ofani
          exposur        econsti        nofanim
          eexposurea     reconstit      onofanima
         heexposurea dreconstitu ionofanimag
        theexposureandreconstitutionofanimage
         heexposurea dreconstitu ionofanimag
          eexposure      reconsti       tonofanima
          exposur        econsti        nofanim
          xposu          const          ofani
          pos            ons            fan
           o              n              a
```

A question worth considering is whether "hologrammer" is (still) an example of fragmentary writing or whether a threshold has been crossed, especially when one contrasts the geometrical form of Riddell's poem with the random typography of cummings's "NO THANKS. NO. 13." In *Typewriter Art: A Modern Anthology* (Tullet 2014: 76), the images formed by overprinting tend to obliterate the alphabet, as in Robert Zend's "Typescape #7" (1978):

TYPESCAPE #7   April 13,1978

URIBURUS   13-4-78
(The first Uriburu is hungry, the second is fulfilled, the third is eating its own tail. ((Uriburu: mythological serpent — the symbol of the universe — which constantly renews itself by destroying itself.)))

More interesting, perhaps, would be Christian Bök's *Crystallography* (2003: 20–21), with its recourse to the self-replicating fragments of fractal geometry:

FRACTAL GEOMETRY

Fractals are haphazard maps
that entrap entropy in tropes.
Fractals tell their raconteurs
to counteract at every point
the contours of what thought
recounts (a line, a plot): recant
the chronicle that cannot coil
into itself—let the story stray
off course, its countless details,
pointless detours, all en route
toward a tour de force, where
the here & now of nowhere is.

A-FRACTAL.

Of course, fractal geometry is distinctively nonlinear ("pointless detours"). Is this true of Bök's "A-FRACTAL"?

More to the point, perhaps, would be the Brazilian Noigandres group, especially the brothers Haroldo and Augusto de Campos, who think of themselves as taking up where Ezra Pound's (or e. e. cummings's) typewriter left off. Here is one of Augusto's texts from 1957, a poem of echoes (of both sight and sound):

                    uma vez
                       uma vala
                          uma foz
                uma vez   uma bala
             uma fala   uma voz
          uma foz   uma vala
       uma bala   uma vez
          uma voz
             uma vala
                uma vez. (E. Williams 1967: n.p.)

And here is a poem (1955) by Haroldo, with the Portuguese version, "si len
cio" (verso) echoed by his French translation, "silence ou phénoménologie de
l'amour" (recto):

Si   Si

    marsupialamor mem   marsupialamour mam
    itos de tam   elle de lam
    prèias prêdod cam   proie   prise   can
    ino am   in am
    or   our
    turris de tolis   tour de talis
    man   man
    gu (LEN)   gu (L E N T)
    tural aman   tural aman
    te em te   t   en   té
    nebras febras   nèbras   fièvre
    de febr   de   fevr
    uário fe   ier   fem
    mural mor   oral   mor
    tálamo   t'   thalamus   t'
    aurifer   auriféroce
    oz : e   noces : et
    foz   bout
    paz   chut
    ps   paix
            CIO   CE.

                              (E. Williams 1967: n.p.)

The idea perhaps is to experience the mobility of these words as well as to see them as fixed in space. In "Pilot Plan for Concrete Poetry" (1958), Haroldo de Campos writes (2007: 208):

> Concrete poetry: tension of word-things in space-time. Dynamic structure: multiplicity of concomitant movements. Thus in music—by definition, an art of timing—space intervenes (Webern and his followers: Boulez and Stockhausen; concrete and electronic music); in visual arts—spatial, by definition—time intervenes (Mondrian and his *Boogie-Woogie* series; Max Bill; Albers and perceptive ambivalence; concrete art in general).

A "multiplicity of concomitant movements," as in complex systems.

VII

Doubtless it will be asked why I have been avoiding the word "collage," or "constellation" (see Perloff 1986: 42–79, on "The Invention of Collage").

The Canadian poet derek beaulieu (Dobson 2013: 69): "I view poetry, as typified by concrete poetry, as the architecturing of the material of language: the unfamiliar fitting together of fragments, searching for structure." The poem below is from beaulieu's "Silence (*C'est mon Dada*)" (beaulieu 2010: 226). On a certain view, one could view the poem as a space-time arrangement whose letters are fixed in place, to be sure, but that at the same time exhibit the kind of mobility that Mallarmé (1992: 305–6, 1965b: 203) imagined words to achieve when freed from syntax and other lexical and grammatical regimens:

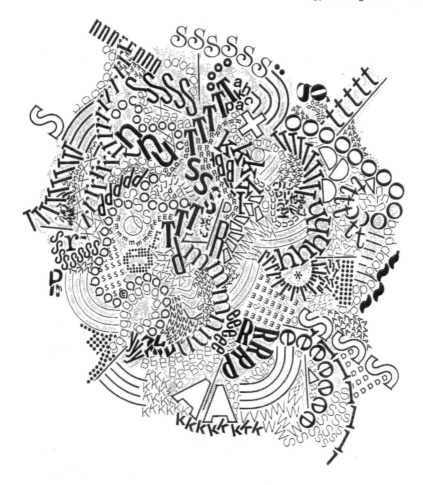

One could argue further that the multiple circularities, not to say complexity, of beaulieu's poem gives the piece a turbulence that linear sequences, like grids, keep under control—which is perhaps why circles are comic (as in cartwheels and merry-go-rounds), whereas straight lines are serious, as is vaudeville's classic straight man with his straight face (which is, nevertheless, comic in the incongruous form of the "deadpan"). The poem's straight lines disappear into its swirling structure, with its random distribution of letters and multiple variations of typeface, and are in any event vastly outnumbered by curves and bends.

However, imagine Mallarmé reading (or regarding) beaulieu's poem a second time: "Very impressive. A compact piece of work, its pieces woven intricately into a whole. But also regressive insofar as it relegates the white space of the page once more to the background. The poem is centripetal rather than centrifugal—one pictures a vortex sucking letters, lines, marks and squiggles (and even an asterisk) into a draining pool of ink."

Consider, by contrast, the following page from Johanna Drucker's *Stochastic Poetics* (2013a: n.p.):

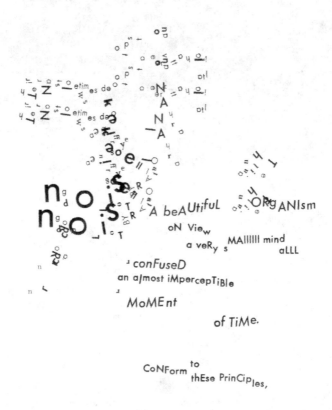

Stochastic Poetics is a book of some forty typographic poems modeled on a stochastic or chaotic system in which sequences of linguistic variables are put into unpredictable play. The poems are made of fragments of found texts ranging from Aristotle's *Poetics* to contemporary chaos theory but including as well street signs and other verbivocovisual events taking place on a certain day on Hollywood Boulevard (a few blocks east of the Chinese Theater) in Los Angeles. In the afterword (2013a: n.p.) Drucker says that the book was inspired by a poetry reading at the L.A.C.E. (Los Angeles Contemporary Exhibitions) in the summer of 2010 "in which the swarms of people milling in and out, the traffic flow from curb to gallery, and the sheer noise and chaos level in the space were all so overwhelming that the poetry reading could barely be heard."

"**nois**e"
"Unity / and a sense / of the WhoLe / is LOST."

In an unpublished paper delivered at the Poetry and Poetics Workshop at the University of Chicago, November 8, 2012, Drucker writes:

> The poems in the piece are pastiche works, culled and gleaned from readings and events, reworked in the composing stick, and then altered in the lock-up on the press. The book is set entirely by hand, in letterpress. No two copies of *Stochastic Poetics* are alike. . . . Each sheet went through the press numerous times and the placement, while not random, was not controlled by any register marks or jigs. So the dynamic effect on the pages differs depending on how the sheets fell. Every bit of the book is set in letterpress, with metal spacers for justification and lock-up. No plaster, adhesives, or other non-traditional materials were used in the production. (See also Drucker 1984: 8–16)

"No two copies of *Stochastic Poetics* are alike": recall (again) Schlegel on the poem of becoming or incompletion: a "stochastic" (variable, chaotic) piece is less an aesthetic object than an event or even series of events—a plurality of mobile pieces rather than a self-same totality.

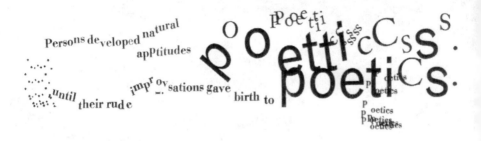

Algorithmic versions
unfiltered
words and threads
whole data search
NOT   allowed to travel

Almost eight and time for the first reader.

id the dealers and twins unnamed
irls are things
ble strings   social stuff
of the world underclass

Persons developed natural apPtitudes until their rude improvsations gave birth to

Start with a point in the BASIN of aTTractIOn
then simplX plot its suBsequent OrbIIITTTTssssssss

VIII

Whence, logically and historically, the next step would take us into the hyper-textual world of digital poetry in which one changes the text of a poem as one moves through the virtual space it inhabits.[14]

But how does one cite a hypertext?

So instead let me conclude my inventory by citing one of Paul Celan's late poems (from *Lichtzwang* [1970]), whose paratactic form, the mismatching of subjects and predicates, returns us to the regulating idea of the fragmentary:

Klopf die	Knock off the
Lichtkeile weg:	bolts of light:
das schwimmende Wort	the dusk
hat der Dämmer.	has the swimming word.

(Celan 1983, 2: 268, 1986: 40–41; trans. slightly amended)

Although my favorite remains the poem with seven wheels—one of Celan's most comic assemblies:

ST
Ein Vau, pf, in der That
Schlägt, mps
Ein Sieben-Rad:
o
oo
ooo
O. (1983, 3: 136)

2

The Impossible Experience of Words

The Later Fiction of Maurice Blanchot and Samuel Beckett

[Thomas] perceived all the strangeness there was in being observed by a word as if by a living being, and not simply by one word, but by all the words that were in that word, by all those that went with it and in turn contained other words, like a procession of angels opening out into the infinite to the very eye of the absolute.
—Maurice Blanchot, *Thomas l'obscur*

My purpose in this chapter is to pursue in some philological detail the symmetries between Samuel Beckett's fiction, particularly one of his later fragmentary writings, and Maurice Blanchot's theory (and practice) of writing as a kind of limit-experience, where writing (among other interminable events: waiting, suffering, dying) is not the work of an agent exercising conceptual control but, as in the epigraph above, an experience of subjection to the material autonomy of words.[1] In an essay on "L'expérience-limite" (1962) Blanchot writes:

> We live [each of the events that is ours] one time as something we comprehend, grasp, bear, and master. . . . We live it another time as something that escapes all employ and all end [*ce qui se dérobe à tout emploi et à toute fin*], and more, as that which escapes our very capacity to undergo it, but whose trial we cannot escape. Yes, as though impossibility, that by which we are no longer able to be able [*cela en quoi nous ne pouvons plus pouvoir*], were waiting for us behind all that we live, think, and say. (1969: 306–7, 1993a: 207)

My thought is that Beckett's fictions are comic derivations of Blanchot's dilemma—the experience of impossibility, of being "no longer able to be able."[2]

Here, for example, is Beckett's Unnamable, in what Blanchot would call the weakness of his "*solitude essentielle*" (1955: 13–32, 1982: 21–34):

> All this business of a labour to accomplish, before I can end, of words to say, a truth to recover, in order to say it, before I can end. . . . All lies. I have nothing to do, that is to say nothing in particular. I have to speak. Whatever that means. Having nothing to say, no words but the words of others, I have to speak. (1965: 314)

"I have to speak," and he may be speaking still. Blanchot, more soberly, describes the dilemma as follows:

> The writer's mastery is not in the hand that writes, the "sick" hand that never lets the pencil go—that can't let go because what it holds doesn't really hold; what it holds belongs to the realm of shadows, and it's itself a shade. Mastery always characterizes the other hand, the one that doesn't write and is capable of intervening at the right moment and put it aside. Thus mastery consists in the power to stop writing, to interrupt what is being written, thereby restoring to the present instant its rights, its decisive trenchancy. (1955: 19, 1982: 25)

The "power to stop writing"! So much, one might say, for the classical ideal of the master craftsman for whom art (*techné*) is a repertoire of models and rules for producing an immortal object of truth and beauty. In Blanchot's account we are given instead a schoolmaster who puts a stop to the unruly or accurséd hand. Imagine mastery as a kind of *prophylaxis*, as if speaking or writing were a chronic disorder or an affliction to be prevented, there being no cure—except, if that is how it is, that of laughter:

> For the likes of us and no matter how we are recounted there is more nourishment in a cry nay a sigh torn from one whose only good is silence or in speech extorted from one at last delivered from its use than sardines can ever offer. (Beckett 1964: 143)

I. *L'malheur de l'écriture*

For Maurice Blanchot, at any rate, the affliction (*l'malheur*) is threefold:

(1) From the French poet Mallarmé Blanchot developed the idea that, unlike the language of everyday speech, the language of writing is not a
"power . . . at our disposal; there is in it nothing we can use. It is never
the language I speak" (1955: 55, 1982: 51).[3] Language is not an instrument; it is irreducible to any function of mediation, any *work* in behalf
of meanings, statements, descriptions, narrations, expressions of feeling, or objects of this or that form or definition. It is rather a material
that exposes me to the limits of my power. In writing I am no longer an
agent but now an utterly passive subject, an abjection exposed to a kind
of pure exteriority, an outside to which no inside or wayside corresponds.
(1955: 357–62, 1982: 163–70)

(2) A "pure exteriority": Following Kafka, Blanchot situates the writer in a
space (*l'espace littéraire*) that is not a place one might inhabit but a surface across which one wanders endlessly like an outlaw or exile (or like
Beckett's Molloy). Writing is a nomadic movement in which there is no
possibility of arrival. In an essay on "Kafka et la littérature" (1949), Blanchot puts it in the form of a characteristic paradox:

> It is as if the possibility that my writing represents exists essentially to
> express its own impossibility—the impossibility of writing that consti-
> tutes my sadness [*ma douleur*]. Not only can it not be put it in paren-
> theses, or accommodate it without destroying it or being destroyed by
> it, but it really is possible only because of its impossibility. (1949: 27–
> 28, 1995: 20)

It is as if the writer belonged to an errant temporality—an *entretemps*—that neither begins nor ends. In one of Kafka's diary entries we read: "It is not death,
alas, but the eternal torments of dying" (1949: 302). Imagine, as Blanchot does,
"the loss of the power to die, the loss of death as power and possibility. . . . To
read the word death *without* negation is to withdraw from it the cutting edge
of decision and the power to negate; it is to cut oneself off from possibility and
the true, but also from death as a true event. It is to surrender to the indistinct
and the undetermined, to the emptiness anterior to events, where the end has
all the heaviness of starting over" (1955: 325, 1982: 142).

(3) Just so. Writing, Blanchot says, is *"l'interminable, l'incessant"* (1955: 20,
1982: 16). It is not a task that one might take up or put down. On the contrary, it is an obligation that one can neither elude nor satisfy. Blanchot

calls it "a sovereign exigency," and again: "an imperious and empty demand [*exigence impérieuse et vide*] exerted all of the time" (1955: 60, 1982: 54–55): an exigency to which one must respond without, however, having any power to do so. No more can one explain the origin (*arché*) or point (*telos*) of such an obligation; that is, like writing, there is no metaphysics that can justify it.

II. *Je n'ai rien à dire*

This aporia dates from the earliest of Blanchot's critical writings (1941–43, for the *Journal des débats*), where the writer is a figure far removed from the philosophical tradition of a disengaged punctual ego exercising rational control over itself and whatever comes before it. Instead he (*il*: he/it: a neutral subject—no one: *personne*) belongs to a decidedly French-Nietzschean tradition in which, in Georges Bataille's words, "experience [is] a voyage to the end of the possible of man" (1988: 7).[4] In his book on Nietzsche (1945) Bataille writes: "If possibility is given us in chance (and isn't received from outside but is the possibility that we are, the possibility that forces us to take risks by forcing us to the very end) there clearly isn't anything of which it could be said, 'It will be possible like this.' It won't be possible but risked. And chance or risk assumes what is impossible" (1992: 104).

As if experience suspended the law of noncontradiction, which is a law of passage that leads somewhere, or is productive of something: concepts, propositions, judgments, self-identity, integrated systems, not to mention "conditions of possibility." Blanchot refuses this law at every turn: he thinks and writes in contradictions—a practice that derives from his critique of Hegel's dialectic of negation, which annihilates the singularity of things by subsuming them into a system of universals free of historical dissonance.[5] For example, in his introduction to his first book of critical essays, appropriately entitled *Faux pas* (1943), Blanchot likens the writer to "a hemiplegic who finds in the same illness both the obligation to walk and the prohibition of walking" (1943: 10, 2001: 2). Or, much to the same point (or impasse):

> The writer finds himself in the increasingly ludicrous condition of having nothing to write, of having no means with which to write it, and of being constrained by the utter necessity of always writing it. Having nothing to express must be taken in the most literal way. Whatever he would like to say,

it is nothing. The world, things, knowledge are to him only landmarks across the void And he himself is already reduced to nothing. (1943: 11, 2001: 3)

The *will to power* turned against itself: writing is no longer a possibility but still an inescapable responsibility (a sentence to be served). Against all reason, the inability to write entails an inability to stop writing. And to add to this complexity: as in the case of Mallarmé, writing annihilates the one who writes, but with this difference, that the writer's disappearance leaves no work in its wake. The writer is "destroyed in an act that puts him into play. The exercise of this ability forces him to immolate this ability. The work that he creates signifies that no work is created. The art he uses is an art in which perfect success and complete failure must appear at once, the fullness of means and their irremediable degeneration, the reality and nothingness of results" (Blanchot 1943: 15, 2001: 5). Later, in one of his essays from the 1960s ("L'absence de livre"), Blanchot will coin the term *désœuvrement* (worklessness, unworking) to describe this useless expenditure of energy (1969: 622, 1993a: 424). But in 1943 the concept (if that is what it is) is already fully in place in the image of "pages made up of a discontinuous series of words" (1943: 16, 2001: 8): in short, the *fragment*, which for Blanchot is not a part separated from a whole but a discourse of interruptions.

III. ". . . that terrible materiality of the word surface . . ."

Samuel Beckett,[6] for his part, belongs very much to this paradoxical milieu—as a principal figure in its history. Consider those famous dialogues with Georges Duthuit:

B.—The only thing disturbed by the revolutionaries Matisse and Tal Coat is a certain order on the plane of the feasible.
D.—What other plane can there be for the maker?
B.—Logically none. Yet I speak of an art turning from it in disgust, weary of its puny exploits, wearying of pretending to be able, of being able, of doing a little better the same old thing, of going a little further down a dreary road.
D.—And preferring what?
B.—The expression that there is nothing to express, nothing with which to express, nothing from which to express, no power to express, no desire to express, together with the obligation to express.[7] (1949: 98; rpt., Beckett 1984: 139)

Whence the Unnamable's impasse (to speak only of him for now):

> The fact would seem to be, if in my situation one may speak of facts, not only that I shall have to speak of things of which I cannot speak, but also, which is even more interesting, but also that I, which is if possible even more interesting, that I shall have to, I forget, no matter. At the same time I am obliged to speak. I shall never be silent. Never.[8] (1965: 291)

What to say, how to say it, under such conditions? As in Blanchot's case, the first step is to suspend the law of noncontradiction, or at all events to experience its absence: "I seem to speak, it is not I, about me, it is not about me. These few general remarks to begin with. What am I to do, what shall I do, what should I do, in my situation, how proceed? By aporia pure and simple? Or by affirmations and negations invalidated as uttered, or sooner or later" (1965: 291). What follows, as if to fill the empty time, are stories of afflicted creatures (avatars of the Unnamable named Mahood and Worm), as well as references to (among other things) a "voice"—"It issues from me, it fills me, it clamours against my walls, it is not mine, I can't stop it, I can't prevent it, from tearing me, racking me, assailing me. It is not mine, I have none, I have no voice and must speak, that is all I know" (1965: 307).

One could say that, like Blanchot, Beckett raises contradiction to the level of a poetic principle whose task is to materialize language, which is, after all, what *The Unnamable* is chiefly about—that is, what the Unnamable, and in turn Beckett's reader, experiences: "I'm in words, made of words, others' words, what others, the place too, the air, the walls, the floor, the ceiling, a world, the whole world is here with me, I'm the air, the walls. . . . I'm all these words, all these strangers, this dust of words, with no ground for their settling" (1965: 386). Words arrive from nowhere, to no purpose, without direction, and without result. They follow one upon another according to a principle of randomness, a principle that is, in principle, self-defeating: "Someone speaks, someone hears, no need to go any further. . . . It goes on by itself, it drags on by itself, from word to word, a labouring whirl, you are in it somewhere, everywhere" (1965: 402).

A "labouring whirl": as if language were structured like the weather, producing the turbulence of chaos theory—or "catastrophe," for short. Imagine words materializing like a storm, a siege or obsession before which writing (and, in the bargain, reading) is without recourse or resource: an abject responsibility incapable of closure.[9]

IV. "... *rien n'est dit* ..."

Coincidentally, while Beckett was composing *L'innomable* (1953), Blanchot was at work on *Celui qui ne m'accompagnait pas* (1953), whose narrator confronts the task of writing, evidently compelled to do so by the presence of another—a clandestine (unnamable) companion who, it turns out, is simply a neutral version of the narrator himself, a *je* mirrored as an *il*: he/it, neither one nor the other. (Even of himself the narrator says: "I was almost no one" [1953: 128, 1993b: 68].)[10] But such writing produces not a *work* but only an obsessive/compulsive experience of words. The narrator finds, for example, that he "became afraid of words, and . . . wrote fewer and fewer of them, even though the pressure exerted inside myself to make me write them soon became dizzying" (1953: 10–11, 1993b: 3). And so he proceeds, if "proceeds" is the word when writing, as the Unnamable understood, is without passage ("Forward! That's soon said. But where is forward?" [Beckett 1964: 368]):

> I could recall, as an intoxicating navigation, the motion that had more than once driven me toward a goal, toward a land that I did not know and was not trying to reach, and I did not complain that in the end there was neither land nor goal, because, in the meantime, by this very motion, I had lost my memory of the land. I had lost it, but I had also gained the possibility of going forward at random [*au hasard*], even though, in fact, consigned to this randomness, I had to renounce the hope of ever stopping. (Blanchot 1953: 18, 1993b: 7)

"Randomness," that is (etymologically), *runaway* words "going forward at random," chiefly by way of fragments of conversation with a *doppelgänger*, who repeatedly asks, "Are you writing? Are you writing at this moment?" (1953: 102, 1993b: 54). As if the task of the other were to keep the narrator at his impossible task—

> "Talk, describe things."
> Which was enough to awaken a spirit of uncertainty.
> "Why describe?" I asked him. "There's nothing to describe, there's almost nothing left." (1953: 112–13, 1993b: 59)

Whence the narrative, so far from "going forward," wanders in a circle: "And I can't think of breaking this circle, I don't think of it because I belong to this circle, and it is possible, in fact, that I'm not writing, because I can't" (1953: 120, 1993b: 64).

What it comes down to, again, is a siege of words: "It was the need to *pacify* those words, suspend for a moment their agitated flight through the house, bring them back, also, to themselves by keeping them away from the feverish earth, that obliged me to ask myself if I shouldn't write—now" (1953: 133, 1993b: 70–71). Writing, as elsewhere in Blanchot, is a reversal of subjectivity in which the writer becomes an instrument, not an ability but an availability— a weakness overcome by what Blanchot, in an essay on Mallarmé's "Le Mystère dans le lettres" (1946), "the strength of an impersonal speech, the subsistence of *a language that speaks itself on its own*"—without, however, disclosing anything but its own implacable density (1949: 62, 1995: 57):

> To say that I understand these words [*ces paroles*] would not be to explain to myself the dangerous peculiarity [*étrangeté*] of my relations with them. Do I understand them? I do not understand them, properly speaking, and they too who partake of the depth of concealment [*la dissimulation*] remain without understanding. But they don't need understanding in order to be uttered [*pour se prononcer*], they do not speak, they are not interior, they are, on the contrary, without intimacy, being altogether outside, and what they designate engages me in the "outside" of all speech [*ce dehors de toute parole*], apparently more secret and more interior than the speech of the innermost heart [*la parole du for intérieur*], but, here, the outside is empty, the secret is without depth, what is repeated is the emptiness of repetition, it doesn't speak, and yet it has always been said already. (1953: 135–36, 1993b: 72)

In the end there is nothing to say because the words that impose themselves are "unconnected, motionless around me though wandering [*quoique errantes*]" (1953: 142, 1993b: 75), leaving nothing behind, unless it is "a suffocating apprehension, the anxious feeling the word 'forgetfulness' brings with it" (1953: 149, 1993b: 79).

V. *Parole de fragment*

Words: "unconnected, motionless."

In 1969 Blanchot gathered together a number of his essays under the title *L'entretien infini* (*The Infinite Conversation*), which begins with a series of fragments of narrative and dialogue that introduce a nameless but characteristically aged (or ageless) interlocutor who *"has lost the power to express himself in a continuous manner"* (1969: xxii–xxiii, 1993a: xxi).[11] And, as if speaking in behalf (or in place) of this interlocutor, many of the essays that follow attempt to gain some purchase on what Blanchot, in "Parole de fragment" ("The Fragment Word"), calls

> A new kind of arrangement not entailing harmony, concordance, or reconciliation, but that accepts disjunction or divergence as the infinite center from out of which, through speech, relation is to be created: an arrangement that does not compose but juxtaposes, that is to say, leaves each of the terms that come into relation *outside* one another, respecting and preserving this *exteriority* and this distance as the principle—always already undercut [*toujours déjà destitué*]—of all signification. Juxtaposition and interruption here assume an extraordinary force of justice. Here all freedom finds its order on the basis of the (uneasy) case it accords us. An arrangement at the level of disarray. An immobile becoming. (1969: 453, 1993a: 308)

"An immobile becoming [*Devenir d'immobilité*]": The ancients are thought to have distinguished between two kinds of time—the time of Chronos, which proceeds consecutively, and the time of *Aion*, which pauses interminably.[12] In "Le grand refus" (1959), Blanchot figures it as a time of impossibility, of which there are several traits, in the first of which "time changes direction, no longer offering itself out of the future as what gathers by going beyond; time, here, is rather the dispersion of a present that, even while being only passage that does not pass [*la dispersion du présent qui ne passe, tout en n'étant que passage*], never fixes itself in a present, refers to no past and goes toward no future: *the incessant*" (1969: 64–65, 1993a: 45).

This is the immobility that Blanchot's *L'attente, l'oubli* (1962) explores, not only with its disjunctive narrative of a "conversation" between a man and a woman whose words hang mostly in suspension between them but especially in its paradoxical wordplay:

> • Attendre, seulement attendre. L'attente étrangère, égale en tous ses moments comme l'espace en tous ses points, pareille à l'espace, exerçant la même pression continue, ne l'exerçant pas. L'attente solitaire, qui était en nous et maintenant passée au dehors, attente de nous sans nous, nous forçant à

attendre hors de notre propre attente, ne nous laissant plus rien à attendre. D'abord l'inimité, d'abord l'ignorance de l'intimité, d'abord le côte à côte d'instants s'ignorant, se touchant et sans rapport. (1962: 31)

• To wait, only wait. Waiting, strange, equal in all of its moments as space is in all of its points, similar to space, exerting the same continuous pressure, not exerting it. Lonely waiting, which was in us and has now passed to the outside, waiting for us without us, forcing us to wait outside our own waiting, leaving nothing to wait for. At first intimacy, at first ignorance of intimacy, at first ignorant moments side by side, touching and without relation.[13] (1997: 14)

The fragment turns reading itself into a kind of waiting by its refusal (or inability) to come to a point, proceeding as it does by way of serial contradictions ("touching and without relation"). In the bargain it makes all of us players in the book's interminable (infinite) conversation, with its refractory imperative: "Exprimer cela seulement qui ne peut être. Le laisser inexprimé (Express only that which cannot be expressed. Leave it unexpressed)" (1962: 35, 1997: 16).

Likewise with respect to forgetting: "Forgetting without the possibility of forgetting. Forgetting forgotten without forgetting" (1962: 147, 1997: 78). And as with waiting and forgetting, so with speaking—once more (by this time perhaps obsessively) an experience of impossibility:

∴ Voulant et ne pouvant parler; ne le voulant pas et ne pouvant se dérober à la parole; alors, parlant-ne parlant pas, dans un même movement que son interlocuteur avait le devoir de soutenir.

Parlant, ne voulant pas; le voulant, ne le pouvant pas.

∴ Wanting to and not being able to speak; not wanting to and not being able to evade speech; thus speaking not speaking, in an identical movement that her interlocutor had the duty to maintain.

Speaking, not wanting to, wanting to, not being able to. (1962: 93, 1997: 48)

VI. What When Words Gone

Paradoxically, in his later works—*Le pas au delà* (1973) and *L'écriture du désastre* (1980)—Blanchot writes about the fragmentary in the classical form of the *pensée*: "Lassitude before words is also the desire for words separated from each other [*le désir des mots espacés*]—with their power, which is meaning, broken, and their composition too, which is syntax or the system's continuity (provided the system be in some way complete in advance and the present a *fait accompli*)" (1980: 18–19, 1986: 8).

Meanwhile in his late fictions—"Company" (1980), "Ill Seen Ill Said" (1981), and "Worstward Ho" (1983)—Beckett takes Blanchot's fragmentary aesthetic to the extreme limits of lassitude. These are, like *The Unnamable* and *How It Is*, extracted utterances—words or voices that overtake, define, and deplete the subjects that suffer them.[14]

Let me conclude by reading *Worstward Ho*, which one might construe as a thought experiment in which the imperative voice finds itself (or its other, "the voice of us all") slowly deprived, not just of things, but of words—words reduced to paratactic intervals of white space where they find a certain freedom or autonomy in their juxtapositions:

> On. Say on. Be said on. Somehow on. Till nohow on. Said nohow on.
> Say for be said. Missaid. From now say for be missaid.
> Say a body. Where none. No mind. Where none. That at least. A place.
> Where none. For the body. To be in. Move in. Out of. Back into. No. No
> out. No back. Only in. Stay in. On in. Still.
> All of old. Nothing else ever. Ever tried. Ever failed. No matter. Try again.
> Fail again. Fail better. (1983b: 8)

A body, a place—as it happens, the familiar figures of an old man, a young boy, and an old woman in a "dim void"—but what had earlier been merely "ill seen, ill said" is now "misseen, missaid," as in a self-canceling system (the law of non-contradiction suspended in a "Thenceless thitherless there"):

> A place. Where none. A time when try see. Try say. How small. How vast.
> How if not boundless bounded. Whence the dim. Not now. Know better
> now. Unknow better now. Know only no out of. No knowing how know
> only no out of. Into only. Hence another. Another place where none. Wither
> whence no return. No. No place but the one. None but the one where none.
> Whence never once in. Beyondless. Thenceless there. Thitherless there.
> Thenceless thitherless there. (11)

"None but the one where none": a failure of logic at which only words can succeed:

> Whose words? Ask in vain. Or not in vain if say no knowing. No saying. No words for him whose words. Him? One. No words for one whose words. One? No words for it whose words. Better worse so. (16)

Words—*its* words, that is, no one's words: "How almost true they sometimes almost ring. How wanting in inanity" (20).[15] So things could be worse, and worse still—for example, "What when words gone?" that is, what then when there are "no words for what when words gone" (28)?

That remains to be seen, or "misseen" (as we shall see).

For the most part the failure of words is, like waiting and dying (or writing), an "incessant, interminable" event made of nonfinite verbs like "worsening," as in—

> Worsening words whose unknown. Whence unknown. At all costs unknown. Now for to say as worst they may only they only they. Dim void shades all they. Nothing save what they say. Somehow say. Nothing save they. What they say. Whosesoever whencesoever say. As worst they may fail ever worse to say. (29)

Just so, as Heidegger remarks in one of his lectures on language, we only really experience words when they fail us.[16] Which is certainly one reason why in *Worstward Ho* words occupy so much of the attention of "whosesoever" says them, as if there were no more voices, only a mind depleted of everything but words:

> Remains of mind then still. Enough still. Somewhose somewhere somehow still enough. No mind and words? Even such words. So enough still. Just enough still to joy. Joy! Just enough still to joy that only the. Only! Enough still not to know. Not to know what they say. Not to know what it is the words it says say. Says? Secretes. Say better worse secretes. What it is the words it secretes say. What the so-said void. The so-said dim. (29–30)

At worst the words speak of an unspeakable void, or less worse of a dimness, or less worse still of an old man and child plodding along, but only at intervals: "They, then the words. Back to them now for want of better on and better fail" (31). And back and forth we go between the "misseen, missaid" and the words that in between "blanks" fall just short of having *naught* but themselves to say—having at least enough ("Just enough still to joy") to start what sounds something like a dispute about nothing:

> Worse less. By no stretch more. Worse for want of better less. Lest best. No. Naught best. Best worse. No. Not best worse. Naught not best worst. Less best worse. No. Least. Least best worse. Least never to be naught. Never to naught be brought. Never by naught be nulled. Unnullable least. Say that best worst. With leastening words say least best worse. For want of worser worst. Unlessenable least best worse. (31–2)

In other words, let *naught* not be thought, as Parmenides taught:

> So leastward on. So long as dim still. Dim undimmed. Or dimmed to dimmer still. To dimmost dim. Leastmost in dimmost dim. Utmost dim. Leastmost in utmost dim. Unworsenable worst.
> What words for what then? How almost they still ring. As somehow from some soft of mind they ooze. From it in it ooze. How all but uninane. To last unlessenable least how loath to leasten. For then in utmost dim to unutter leastmost all. (33)

Finally, it comes down to the coming and going of words amid the coming and going of the "shades" of an old man, a child, an old woman, a skull with one or two holes for staring eyes—or worse: "None but the one where none" (42)—leaving just enough words to avoid the void: "A pox on void. Unmoreable unlessable unworseable evermost void" (42–43). One might take Beckett's paradoxical wordplay—"For then in utmost dim to unutter leastmost all"—as a way of letting words be words, materials rather than functions, interruptions of white space ("Blanks for when words gone. When nohow on" [40]) inscribing the impossibility that impelled *Worstward Ho*—and Beckett himself—from the start:

> Nohow less. Nohow worse. Nohow naught. Nohow on.
> Said nohow on. (47)

PART II

3

Dialectrics

Turbulence and Contradiction in J. H. Prynne's *Kazoo Dreamboats*

*The unpretentious thing evades thought most stubbornly. Or can it be
that this self-refusal of the mere thing, this self-contained independence,
belongs precisely to the nature of the thing?*
—Martin Heidegger, "The Origin of the Work of Art"

*The concept of resistance may provide an alternative criterion of
intelligibility; one which does not undermine the "presence, actuality, and
existence" of an object or person, but which makes accessible the fact of
its existence without impairing its status as a substantial, independent
entity.*
—J. H. Prynne, "Resistance and Difficulty"

I. *Désœuvrement*

Perhaps the first thing one might say about J. H. Prynne's recent *Kazoo Dreamboats; or, On What There Is*, is that its absence of line breaks marks a departure
from the predominantly versified forms gathered together in his *Poems*. Here
is *Kazoo*'s opening sentence:

> Along the corridor of near frequency I saw willing and discrete
> the season not yet for sorrow advanced, nearby not yet even so
> inference to claim. (2011: 5)

There are, to be sure, two prose pieces that Prynne included in his *Poems*: "A
Note on Metal" (1968) and "The *Plant Time Manifold* Transcripts" (c. 1973). And
Kazoo's way of putting words together continues the paratactic procedures of

Prynne's later poetry.[1] But when paragraphs replace pentameters the force of disjunction seems all the more powerful:

> We'll make folly in pledge to stem-division as
> decisive cut for cut across narrows, passage throat offensive
> in try once only or by defiance vectors, filmic particle mist de-
> graded not yet conjugate in mission. Always desired by zero option
> wide-eyed node employ cloud droplets *en masse* phantasmal, near in to
> scar friable distinct cash-back nexus, on the plate. What's to
> be got contagious *dendrite* hit conductance ran fast even flash-like,
> punished in stupid glory by ever the same to say. (5; my emphasis)

For the record: in the subatomic world the term "dendrite" refers to the frazzled branches of a neuron, comparable perhaps to the frazzled lines of this passage—except that dendrites are "contagious": they conduct electricity ("fast even flash-like") in variable directions, whereas *parataxis* is the trope of interruption: "Passage throat offensive / in try once only."

We might call *Kazoo Dreamboats* a "poem in prose," or maybe a work that is neither "poetical" nor discursive but "nongeneric." The French often speak simply of *l'écriture*: writing that is neutral with respect to concepts, categories, and distinctions. I am reminded (again) of Maurice Blanchot's term for the fragmentary assembly: *désœuvrement* (worklessness), "an arrangement that does not compose but juxtaposes, that is to say, leaves each of the terms that come into relation *outside* one another, respecting and preserving this *exteriority* and this distance as the principle—always already undercut—of all signification."[2]

II. Fair Fields of Turbulence

However, call the thing what you will, the important question is not aesthetic (what is it?) but philological: How might one read it? Some purchase on this question may be gained from the fact that *Kazoo* is, whatever else it is, a work of citations—and it is so even more abundantly than are many of Prynne's poems, which frequently ring with the echoes and epigraphs of a polymath's library.[3] Not only are the numerous quotations set off from the main text by scare quotes and indentations, but we are given at poem's end a list of "Reference Cues" that help to identify the poem's chief formal antecedent—William Langland's *Piers Plowman*—as well as the philosophical and scientific concepts that regulate the poem's progress, if one can call it that. For arguably, as the subtitle suggests,

Kazoo Dreamboats is a work of metaphysics in which what the "I" of the poem sees is no longer Langland's famous "fair field full of folk" but a variable series of force fields (electromagnetic, linguistic, and even musical), whose patterns and elements follow models of chaos and complexity rather than any principle of linearity or noncontradiction. Thus, at the very least, one can say that something like a principle of decorum obtains between the *material* resistance of "what there is" and the *material* difficulty of the poem itself:

> A glut run together polishing the wall facing, the metric surface
> non-generic endurance did fancy by entrance if harmful,
> shade upon phosphor passage net agreement cut to a shred. (5)

Certainly, "non-generic endurance" is what Prynne's reader needs: his writing will only answer, if at all, to close attention to its details. Accordingly, what follows will also, of necessity, be citational in its proceedings.

Like *Piers Plowman*, *Kazoo Dreamboats* is a visionary poem, but one whose point of view seems internal to the turbulence of what is seen:

> I saw it upmost, to know partly is by now
> not to unknow else with borrowed light induced by origin perpetual,
> by passion lying flat and tumid for advantage, for all or nothing
> is the play sequence left over. What is enclosed over the time
> lag partition is included also, all by so incremental as fostered
> in acts of next recension. (6)

"I saw it upmost"—but *what is it*, exactly, that the "I" sees? Prynne's prose predicates nothing of it (but not for nothing, as we shall see). Luckily for us, the paragraph introduced by this recondite passage contains a couple of straightforward quotations that may help us to get our bearings. The first reads:

> "We now recognize that 'empty space'
> is a turmoil of electromagnetic waves of all frequencies and wave-
> lengths. They wash through and past us" or say, "we are all bathed
> in this 'vacuum infinity' of virtual electromagnetic waves," pro-
> voked and then quelled in reciprocal perturbation. (6)

Unseen, unfelt, but a turbulent system for all that. The second quotation is as follows:

In all matter there are continuous jostlings of positive and negative charges; at every point in a material body or in a vacuum, transient electric and magnetic fields arise spontaneously. These fluctuations in charge and in field occur not only because of thermal agitation but also because of inescapable quantum-mechanical uncertainties in the positions and momenta of particles and in the strengths of electromagnetic fields. The momentary positions and electric currents of moving charges act on, and react to, other charges and their fields. (7)

The citations are from a book about Van der Waals *forces*, that is, electromagnetic forces that play off of one another ("reciprocal perturbation") instead of stabilizing into any sort of coherence.[4] If we think of gravity as a *strong* force that brings things down to earth where we can take hold of them, Van der Waals forces are *weak*, given, if anything, to turning things loose—picture molecules bouncing freely off one another (like the words below) instead of coalescing into a structure:

> For fields thus filled it was no dream if yet so dear I lay, pronate
> attempered pronoun sounded dear heart how suckled, hot pies! be
> blithe, for birth integer broad alleged awake among the things
> that are, in *spoken footprint* cordial how alike by probe to lit
> shelf grains. (6; my emphasis)

Pause for a moment and contemplate the "spoken footprint." Imagine Crusoe's bewilderment.

III. Contradiction/Nonidentity

At least we can, for a start, conclude that the "I" who *sees* is "not-I," a neutral voice without a history or identity: a "pronate attempered pronoun" awake "among the things that are" but not (strictly) a speaking subject.[5] Better to ask again: What are these "things that are"—these "hot pies" popping up by surprise?

> I sat softly down won with wrong for
> true line up purchase, pair try to shake in full spring leaf refused
> against metal over a rock pavement abraded by parallax in opportunity
> dropped down, in earth flooding, mother admit me by *dielectric* promise
> of this field. (7; my emphasis)

The term "dielectric," which doubles as a pun on "dialectic," points the way. A *dielectric* is, if I understand, an insulator that, unlike a conductor, disrupts or displaces the flow of electric charges through a given material so that what results is, in effect, something like a trackless storm—"continuous jostlings of positive and negative charges"—in marked contrast, for example, to the dialectic of Hegel (and Marx), which defines a history of reason that drives events forward (however explosively) toward some coherent end or purpose.[6]

Kazoo puts it this way:

> The molecule is severally pandemic, indecision
> layered off by step quanta or this or its hit. Win the single atom
> can be considered to have a fluctuating rotating dipole moment,
> nothing changes for this is the self-change of nothing as at sac-
> cadic variance, substantially composed of its moments in transit,
> in the field most winking and unrespected. Get what it is, for who
> is it force fielded, spectra reversed another day older be calm all
> at call to envisage. (8)

A molecule that is "severally pandemic" would be one whose center is everywhere and whose horizon is expanding along variable lines of flight. Likewise an atom with "a fluctuating rotating dipole moment" would send its molecules speeding in every direction. Yet not to worry: "nothing changes for this is the self-change of nothing as at saccadic variance," where "saccadic" is something like rapid eye-movement—perhaps the comically dizzy effort of a literary critic to follow these catastrophic proceedings, which no doubt a physicist would find tedious.

The unquiet ghost in this complex machine is Parmenides, whose "On Nature" (listed in the "Reference Cues") is a prototype of the visionary poem and whose vision of the unchanging repose of Being—"'there is no place void of being, for the void is nothing . . . ; so then being is not moved; it is impossible for it to go anywhere, if there is no void'" (15)—is being turned inside out:

> Nothing that is not nothing will do it, across
> a vacuum referred by its overt container, from inside to side placed
> out interdict risen fortress narrow alert summation vectoral index,
> do alternated position even integral even averaged through time. (8)

"Nothing that is not nothing": $0 \neq 0$.

To illuminate these nothings, *Kazoo* provides a citation from Mao Zedong's essay, "On Contradiction" (1937):

> There is internal contradiction in every single thing, hence its motion and development. Contradictoriness within a thing is the fundamental cause of its development, while its interrelations and interactions with other things are secondary causes. . . . It is evident that purely external causes can only give rise to mechanical motion, that is, to changes in scale or quantity, but cannot explain why one thing changes into another. (8)

Mao of course is thinking of social transformations in which the word "development" has some application, whereas *Kazoo's* vision is of self-interfering systems in which nothing can claim an identity for itself: "I saw seeing itself dissolve" (8), leaving us somewhere in a nowhere, where

> being-itself deletes far out its consisting notational self-
> hood, the nouns illicit as bounded only by neglected as not
> coming or going to be or be relinquished, the inclusion of un-never
> at contradicted mutable edging. (9)

A universe in which contradiction is the only true universal would be self-contradictory: a possible impossible world.[7] So along with a dictionary of *illicit* nouns, imagine a self-deleting universe. And "un-never" is presumably a "forever" that has reached some sort of indeterminate ("contradicted mutable") limit.

Remember that for Parmenides it is impossible for anything not to be. And, moreover, whatever is is what it is without confusion or interruption, whereas *Kazoo* figures being as nonidentical with itself, like Mao's singularity that without warning turns suddenly into something else—a line of thinking that defeats, among other things, any principle of exclusion, which is to say that nothing is forbidden:

> Our morning hymn this is, and
> song at evening echo confuted by shared antagonism, implicit not
> by next coming-to-be as the world is transformed in feature full
> of folk by what is it not, time-locked against spokes in the cycle
> of saying so. Indicative ridiculous also, *won't you come home*
> *Bill Bailey before a toast and tea*, scumbags! reptiles! the old folks
> Just better stay at home or lose their reason too . . . .

I saw no less than these
things right up on peremptory shore line.[8] (9; my emphasis)

The conceit here might bring John Donne back from the dead: "the world is transformed . . . by what is it not, time-locked against spokes in the cycle of saying so," meaning that nothing can gainsay its metamorphosis, variable and perpetual as it may be—all this to the accompaniment of a Dixieland classic and a phrase from T. S. Eliot's "Prufrock," one that seems appropriate to the unstable matter at hand:

> Time for you and time for me,
> And time yet for a hundred indecisions,
> And for a hundred visions and revisions,
> Before the taking of a toast and tea. (1952: 4)

The principle of nonexclusion is without jurisdiction, as we know from earliest modernism.[9] Collage is, after all, an essentially comic form, made of incongruities, and it is (again) coherent with *Kazoo*'s formal freedom:

> Enter the time stream arbitrarily, chance
> by random necessity in its flux at concept of unfinish: the lamp
> decays by renewal. (10)

IV. Polytonality

One could digress here on the topic of entropy, but *Kazoo* hurries itself along, meanwhile sending coherence on its way to the recycling bin:

> Wave good-bye don't be stupid, the location
> is obscure because *coherence is not spatial and is without meaning*
> *beyond its scrap value*, every fly on the wall could tell you this. (11; my
> emphasis)

To assist us in our transport we are given, and not surprisingly at this point, a citation from Alban Berg on the atonal (or, more properly, polytonal) music for his opera *Wozzeck*:

> The scene again attempts to achieve both diversity and unity by subject-
> ing the six-note chord, as had earlier been the case with the single note

and the rhythm, to every possible kind of variation such as partitioning, inversion, redistribution and register changes of the note. . . . Here again the overall structure of the piece is obtained through the use of the traditional symmetry of a ternary form, in that the six-note collection appears at only one transpositional level in the outer parts of the scene (although, obviously, in all varied forms) while in the central section it is transposed to all the other levels of the chromatic scale. (11)

In "Lecture on Wozzeck" (1929), Berg speaks of his "desire for musical variety, for a diversity of patterns," for a serial form of "one thing after another."[10] To which Prynne adds this self-reflexive addendum—

> The play of unity
> as a mental device with denial of its self-image, contracted
> to open a hazard sentence with subject deletion at null point of
> its entry. (11)

—where "a hazard sentence with subject deletion" might be read as a synecdoche for *Kazoo* (or "what there is") as a whole.

Unity, in any case, is not of this world:

> Tongues perplexed by speech of fluid memory in knowledge self-
> made, go for it and better be told, tolling this time be, it is
> necessity in its own embracement. Close to uttered void, unity
> in nothing, else. Window not found. (12)

Instead, "*hysteresis* asserts its full moral latency" (12; my emphasis), meaning roughly that a system, being temporal (or complex), is never at one with itself, is always falling short of itself, or can inhabit (like one's unmoored mind) more than a single state at any given time:

> Thought is free, nede
> ne hath no lawe, from severance or drawn conflation, in the
> limit of close approach liminal not boundary, variance closer
> to its own zero word for word reflected, can 'pay for'
> this mass displacement against gravity. (13)

"Thought is *free*": as Tristram Shandy knew, nothing (not even the gravity of reason) can keep it down, much less on track. Like Berg's polytonal music, it pursues "every possible variation"—as in Gilles Deleuze and Félix Guattari's "nomad aesthetics": "This streaming, spiraling, zigzagging, snaking, feverish line of variation liberates a power of life that human beings had rectified and organisms had confined, and which matter now expresses as the trait, flow, or impulse traversing it" (1987: 499). For Deleuze and Guattari, rationality desires conceptual control, whereas "what is" (like *Kazoo* itself) desires *freedom* to wander and digress—variables in constant variation—even to the point of no return.

V. The Song of Birds That Do Not Sing

It follows that *Kazoo* would have a hole in it if it did not include Heisenberg in its proceedings, where a word can fix anything but what is in flux or at odds with itself ("chance by random necessity"). Hence the "uncertainty principle": the more one knows about where a particle is at any given moment, the less one knows about where or how fast it is moving, much less where to stand with respect to such a thing. A citation puts this more accurately:

> The zero-point fluctuation is an immediate consequence of the uncertainty principle. Observed for a time inverse to its frequency, an electromagnetic mode or degree of freedom has an uncertainty in its corresponding energy, an uncertainty proportional to the time of observation. . . . The language must be able to talk about real materials in which electric fields or charge fluctuations occur, oscillate with natural frequencies of the substance, and die away over time. (14–15)

"The language must be able to talk about real materials," but like every system, language suffers from "hysteresis," always falling behind or stumbling over what it tries to grasp. "Fluctuation" is certainly *Kazoo*'s watchword, but like the void, "it can hardly be spoken of" (15), which perhaps explains why the name of Heraclitus, the first philosopher of fluctuation (and hence "resistance"), is nowhere mentioned, even though his profile shadows the poem at every gap and turn.

A simple case in point is the anomaly of the colorless color. For example, *Kazoo* cites Aristotle's refutation of Parmenides, where the Stagirite defends the multiplicity and heterogeneity of "what is" (*Physics*, Book I: 186, 5–10; see Aristotle 1984: 318):

> In case only whites are considered, white meaning one thing, none the less there are many whites and not one: since neither in the succession of

things nor in the argument will whiteness be one. For what is predicated of white will not be the same as what is predicated of the object which is white, and nothing except white will be separated from the object: since there is no other ground of separation except the fact that the white is different from the object in which the white exists. (Prynne 2011: 15)

To which Aristotle adds: "Hence what just is is not; for it is true to say that it is white, and we found this to mean what is not. So 'white' must also mean what just is; and then 'is' has more than one meaning" (Book I: 186, 10–12; see Aristotle 1984: 318). If "'is' has more than one meaning," that is because whatever "is" (like white) is absolutely singular and irreducible, outside the alternatives of universal and particular. Whether Aristotle would go so far as Mao's motto—"There is internal contradiction in every single thing."—is doubtful, but *Kazoo* speaks merrily of

> The song of birds that do not sing,
> because there are none where else would they sing, not from absence
> nor migrancy, the not-song is from not-being and not merely not
> there nor not-possible nor silentness falling rapt upon attentive
> deaf ears. (15)

We could, in a fit of logic, dismiss this as so much double-talk—

> I saw too by links of redaction in
> fluency, not yet perfect because by nature self-mutable even the
> bounds transient each to alter in replacement through pair logic
> overlay, in otherhood unfinished bearing phrasal turmoil in cap
> position, limit across rotation the corridor not self-invaded
> by sweetness each time in momentary batch flavor. (16)

—but remember that in Prynne's poetics difficulty ("phrasal turmoil") is the mirror of a thing's resistance to predication (*s* is *p*), which is what Mao is all about: "'In given conditions, each of the contradictory aspects within a thing transforms itself into its opposite, changes its position to that of its opposite'" (17). *Kazoo* proceeds accordingly:

> I saw these gaps of explanation rolling like wheels contrary within themselves, alien motions on fire with *coriolis* demeanour. I saw the grains

self-rotate in their own amazement with noise of spheres metallic and burnished, along the baseline it is by amount at principle neither so nor not because contradiction is inherent and not alternate in sense of ordering, I saw this notion in full fiery finesse, alive alive-o. (17; my emphasis)

Gloss: "coriolis" is something like a subsidiary of uncertainty, namely the deflection of moving particles when they are viewed in what physicists call a rotating reference frame (picture the earth spinning on its axis). If only one could see this for oneself, in "full fiery / finesse, alive alive-o," leaving nothing unsung:

> In Dublin's fair city, where the girls are so pretty
> I first set my eyes on sweet Molly Malone
> As she wheeled her wheel-barrow
> Through streets broad and narrow
> Crying cockles and mussels, alive, alive-O!
> Alive, alive-O! alive, alive-O!
> Crying cockles and mussels, alive, alive-O!
> She was a fish-monger, but sure 'twas no wonder
> For so were her father and mother before
> And they each wheeled their barrow
> Through streets broad and narrow
> Crying cockles and mussels, alive, alive-O!
> Alive, alive-O! alive, alive-O!
> Crying cockles and mussels, alive, alive-O!

"Molly Malone" is a nineteenth-century Irish ballad about a seventeenth-century Dublin beauty, who was further commemorated by a statue erected on Grafton Street in Dublin in 1988. The ballad is not music of the spheres, perhaps, but neither is it heavy metal ("noise of the spheres metallic and burnished"). No doubt upscale readers would prefer allusions more literary:

> Still point of a turning world self-deluded in unthought anyone could
> purchase indulgence at cost still nothing even the zero-field is inflected
> by charge and currency. District and Circle from top to below O Bottom
> thou art translated. (17)

But in *Kazoo* the cultural alternatives of "high" and "low" are, like everything else, upended (turn and turn about).

VI. *Entretemps*

As for the continuing *amplificatio* of words:

> The sentence in word build is additive
> but logic partitions the stream, sense outriders thicken its pur-
> pose impossible for anything not to be or not if by its own option
> of necessity, thus it is impossible for anything not to be. That
> state of not being anything is reserved for nothing, heavily in
> occupation. (18)

In other words, anything goes, despite the interventions of logic: even the void is, against all reason, a plenum ("heavily in occupation"). While we are at it, what should we make of this wild sentence?

> By sonic socratic dub nett recusancy obversive deduct interval
> exfold, train up pitch departures, percuss the air punctual let
> addit pressure point, aqueous gearing will screen hyperbaric fully
> virtual it is separation. (18)

Perhaps *Kazoo* answers by reminding us of the comic nature of difficulty:

> These are the markers of what's
> there, what there is, by necessity in the field of self-play and
> no player, deduct mentally. There is a garden in her face when
> owls do cry, or if I live or if I die. (19)

Acute *parataxis* is the poetic equivalent of scientific complexity ("the field of self-play and / no player"), which I take to be the poem's argument, given in the following citation:

> Molecular contradiction given out for taken aback, 'each
> new distribution seems to contradict what preceded it; since there are
> no predictable continuities, *one can only listen in the immediate present to*
> *each moment as it occurs*' (19; my emphasis).

Or, in words to the same effect: "Titration of self-boundary each close to contrary echo, cross-harvest defeat of integration" (19); "Titration" refers to a chemical analysis used to determine the unknown concentration of an alien substance—in water, for example). However it appears,

> Within the span of
> what is, being is previous to life and by negation is the substance
> of itself, what is and what is not conclude the molecular universe. (19)

But note especially: "One can only listen in the immediate present to each moment as it occurs" (19). We could, had we the patience, take this as the rule for reading *Kazoo Dreamboats*.

Interestingly, in place of Heraclitus, we are given Leucippus, a Greek atomist who was at home as much with the empty as with the full and for whom turbulence and complexity are the occasion of "what there is," the whirling from which nothing escapes even while everything comes and goes:

> Worlds or *kosmoi* are formed when groups of atoms combine to form a cosmic whirl, which causes the atoms to separate out and sort by like kind. A sort of membrane of atoms forms out of the circling atoms, enclosing others within it and creating pressure by whirling. The outer membrane continually acquires other atoms from outside when it contacts them, which take fire as they revolve and form the stars, with the sun in the outermost circle. Worlds are formed, grow and perish, according to a kind of necessity. (20–21)

To which *Kazoo* responds at once with the vision of a giant maw:

> Here I saw beyond this to the corridor in assured vacant possession
> telescopic to the field inside the mouth, where speech-parts
> of separation had been swallowed in foreground almost in forgive-
> ness, fricative was the advice and to palate by adhesion said to
> be forward. (21)

Imagine "speech-parts of separation," as in a possible world whose creatures speak a language of disjunctions—no "and," "but," "yet," or "so," but only (at most) adverbs occupying an *entretemps*: between, (. . .), meanwhile—a *dielectric* hiatus that recedes into a past that never was while the future arrives on a different page.[11] As for "fricatives": *frication* is a turbulent flow of air, a hiss, gurgle, or catch, but also something like the sound a kazoo makes—one does not blow into a kazoo, one hums into it from the back of one's throat.

Meanwhile, in the *entretemps*, one might freely assemble a collage of "abraded detritus" (25): (1) postdental hygiene: "bacteria scraped off from words" (21); (2) a few voting reminders: "Rule One: people with top pay are rubbish. . . . Rule Two: Diogenes / offered himself as a master, in the market, to any slave who needed one. Rule Three: you do not see into the life of things, dimensionless or not, except by harvest data plotted against uncertainty. Rule Four: justice is scarce" (21); (3) a Greek aphorism: "Empty truth is a medicine without a sickness" (21); (4) a futile plea: "Come on be direct for a change" (22); (5) an advice column: "Keep very calm since excess along the indigent / indignant border is the radiant bonus paid out against Rule One" (22); (6) a Holocaust scene:

> They all go forward where else I saw them go, then
> one said, I will take the shoes with me, we all trembled and I
> nodded because it was right, burning for burning the shoes had
> been saved for this and now so it was, was to be (23);[12]

(7) followed by a scene from everyday life: "In the morning milk delivery up to the very door clink clink I / heard it on the step, it was Andrew of course our regular" (23); (8) a painted nude; (9) a film clip from World War II: "Bomb the airport burn off the ocean terminal rip out those waves, baby it's time" (24); (10) a ludic lyric:

> Oh then light the
> light, doubt the good fight, bearing up towards illusory
> primordial laundry basket. (24)

Imagine (after Walter Benjamin) a deschooled schoolroom in which "to read" is not to decipher but simply to cite.[13]

VII. The Canny Gaffer Knows

Inevitably, the Kantian question of how knowledge is possible arises from this disjunctive complexity: "All right then how is a dearness of being as other than itself / able to be felt and known . . . [?]" (25). Arises, but only to be superseded by the anarchic question that implicitly regulates Prynne's poem: How can what is singular and nonidentical be at all intelligible in Kant's or any philosopher's terms?[14] Terms, after all, demand concepts. Putting aside its "Cranky-danky fear of abstractions" (26), *Kazoo* frames it this way:

> . . . how can these
> things become those things unless these cross so slant to
> those by syncopation of semblance to be in full self retort,
> chemic valence disputed circuitry. (26)

One might answer that if, on Mao's law of contradiction, being is "in full self retort" (26), it is even less empirically accessible than anything that Langland's visionary sees:

> So then we know
> (or, more conservatively 'expect') that, at zero temperature,
> the spins will be frozen into configurations aligned along some
> (domain-wise) constant magnetisation axis. (26)

In other words, as in Zeno's paradox, singularities in flight should theoretically slow their gambit to the freezing point of self-identity, but (following the rule of *hysteresis*) they forever fall short of arrival:

> The adjunct limbs
> jostle to each other suppletive metric fluctuation closer to
> self-same but never quite, word for word parlance in the milk-
> run acronyms of this day. (26)

Remember the "song of birds that do not sing."

But before concluding, let us give this screw another turn. Maybe we are, after all, and against all reason, in a state analogous to that of negative theology:

> The
> stake-out is clearest at night, in gas-exchange microporous
> what's not seen is true to being so, the spread calculus set
> from ground zero some canny gaffer you bet known to be in
> fibrous cloudy attachment being *in situ* planar slot uppance.
> To be light and bright dilates passion across the full corridor

in profile of what conduces to void, serial negation drainage
of spirit intake, out of the way of the Way. (26)

Blinded (or depleted) as we are by the "light and bright," we could perhaps do worse than let this nocturnal "canny gaffer" be our stand-in and interpreter, someone who can explain what earlier made so little sense:

In the complete structure the whole empty box from
facing without directive is in contradicted within self-agency
anisotropic, needles by deduction or front-seat driven darts dis-
pensed by contrary energetic repulse, of twin-bond confronted by
so-being internally against being itself. (17)

The "complete structure" is, like *Kazoo* itself, *anisotropic* (v. isotropic): that is, nonidentical, with words and things flying like darts "by contrary energetic re-pulse," everything turned "internally against being itself." An ontology of inter-nal contradiction, which grinds philosophy, poetry, and history to dust by set-ting words and things free of comprehension or function.

VIII. The Exit Dream

Kazoo Dreamboats concludes with a citation concerning a cenotaph:

The original cremation pyre was placed where the heavens met the earth
and where the inhabitants of nearby settlements could observe smoke ris-
ing into the air. It was also located in the one place on the hilltop where
the position of a distant mountain would correspond to that of the summer moon. The subsequent development of the site gave monumental expression to this relationship, gradually focusing that particular alignment
until it was narrowed down to the space between the tallest stones.[15] (27)

Strange that a visionary poem transfixed by turbulence and contradiction—

This is and must be the thought of nothing that
cannot be apart from what is, neither as or by cause, what it is
to be, relentless and unsame. (6)

—should end with a "monumental expression" of synchronicity: earth and moon aligned between two stones like a dotted "i." Appropriately, and in keeping with the freewheeling norms of comedy, *Kazoo*'s last words celebrate this synchronicity with a song and dance:

> To be this with sweet
> song and dance in the exit dream, sweet joy befall thee is by
> rotation been and gone into some world of light exchange, toiling
> and spinning and probably grateful, in this song. (27)

4

Metastatic Lyricism

John Wilkinson's Poetry and Poetics

I think well of meaning.
—Gertrude Stein, *Stanzas in Meditation*

I. Mallarmé's Modernism

During the past half century I've returned a number of times to that region of literary modernism occupied originally by the French poet Stéphane Mallarmé, with his idea of a poem purified of everything but the physical (musical, but mainly visual) material of its language. In an essay from 1895, "Crise de vers," Mallarmé writes:

> L'œuvre pure implique la disparation élocutoire du poète, qui cède l'initiative aux mots, par le heurt de leur inégalité mobilisés; ils s'allument de reflets réciproques comme une virtuelle trainée de feux sur des pierreries, remplaçant la respiration perceptible en l'ancient souffle lyrique ou la direction personnelle enthousiaste de la phrase. (1992: 276–77)

> If the poem is to be pure, the poet's voice must be stilled and the initiative taken by the words themselves, which will be set in motion as they meet unequally in collision. And in an exchange of gleams they will flame out like some glittering swath of fire over precious stones, and thus replace the audible breathing in lyric poetry of old—replace the poet's own personal and passionate control of verse. (1956: 40–41)

The poem, in other words, is no longer (as in romantic poetics) the lyrical expression of a subject; it is now an *object* that occupies a space of its own, namely the white space of the printed page, which ceases to be a mere background and becomes instead a field in which typography replaces syntax as a way of holding words together, or perhaps taking them apart, as in this poem by Walter Conrad Arensberg (1878–1954):

ING
Ing? Is it possible to mean ing?
Suppose
     For the termination in *g*
            a disoriented
            series
       of the simple fractures
                in sleep.
                Soporific
       has accordingly a value for soap
              so present to
              sew pieces.
              And *p* says: Peace is.
And suppose the *i*
         to be big in ing
         as Beginning.
            Then Ing is to ing
as aloud
     accompanied by times
and the meaning is a possibility
            of ralsis. (Rothenberg 1974: 4–5)

Ralsis?

II. Schizophrenic Poetics

For a more pressing example, consider this poem by the contemporary British poet, John Wilkinson:

HARMOLODICS
Atom-deep in the mix shall ricochet out & splin-
tering off bass, its force out in the open
     ill-received, distractedly snows:

> Set hand to this for the sharp
> > Left to weep
> Though desolate, he dons obedient smiles
> > which break, playing his face;
> > their parchment clears the decks for rend-
> ition, sounding off where the choral re-
> > Shroud-knot of a cradlesong
> rares sweet & musty   Now get re-choked. (1994: 125)

The poem (appropriately published by a press named Parataxis Editions) continues for a dozen more stanzas, but the first already captures the "dissentience" (that is, the "discord" or "disagreement," among other synonyms) implicit in the poem's title. "Harmolodics" is a term coined by the great jazz saxophonist, Ornette Coleman—a term whose meaning is difficult to pin down but that refers (roughly) to a musical theme played simultaneously but differently by the various members of an ensemble, resulting in something like "heterophony," which one might think of as music (or maybe the sound of words) that falls somewhere between "polyphony" and "cacophony."[1] In any event, the paratactic arrangements of Wilkinson's verse are *heterophonic* precisely because of the way his words form self-interfering combinations—for example, "parchment" as a predicate of a smiling face (!).[2]

Why Wilkinson writes this way—

> sounding off where the choral re-
> > Shroud-knot of a cradlesong
> rares sweet & musty   Now get re-choked:

—and the paradoxical ways in which he accounts for it, form the subject of what follows.

In a famous essay, "Postmodernism, or The Cultural Logic of Late Capitalism," Fredric Jameson adopted Jacques Lacan's notion of schizophrenia to describe this sort of writing—"a breakdown in the signifying chain, that is, the interlocking syntagmatic series of signifiers which constitutes an *utterance* or a meaning" (1984: 71–72). Despite the way Jameson's diagnosis has frequently been taken (and perhaps was even intended), this schizophrenic "experience of pure material Signifiers," where the present disappears into a past that never was and the future never arrives, may not be an altogether bad thing:

> . . . the breakdown of temporality suddenly releases this present of time from all the activities and the intentionalities that might focus it and make it a space of praxis; thereby isolated, that present suddenly engulfs the subject with undescribable vividness, a materiality of perception properly overwhelming, which effectively dramatizes the power of the material— or better still, the literal—Signifier in isolation. This present of the world or material signifier comes before the subject with heightened intensity, bearing a mysterious charge of reality, but which one could just as well imagine in the positive terms of euphoria, the high, the intoxicatory or hallucinogenic intensity. (75)

The materiality of words is an interval of freedom from the rationality of ends and means. But notice especially the last sentence, where the "material signifier" works like a narcotic and reading becomes a hallucinatory transport.

As Theodor Adorno proposes, aesthetic experience, whatever else it is, is a dislocation of the subject: "The shock aroused by important works is not employed to trigger personal, otherwise repressed emotions. Rather, this shock is the moment in which recipients forget themselves and disappear into the work; it is the moment of being shaken" (1997: 244).

Perhaps one way to think of literary modernism is that its goal, or anyhow effect, is the shake-up, even befuddlement, of the reader.

And here perhaps is a context in which to begin addressing the difficulties of John Wilkinson's poetry and poetics. Wilkinson, interestingly, worked for many years as a caregiver in psychiatric medicine and seems in basic agreement with Jameson that in schizophrenia words become objects that achieve "a priority over their signifying function" (2007: 160). But there remains a difference between poetry and pathology, however complex or even indeterminate. In an essay on "Too-Close Reading: Poetry and Schizophrenia" (1998), Wilkinson mounts something like a defense of the "unmodernist" lyricism of John Wieners (1934–2002)—a poet who did in fact suffer from bouts of mental illness— against the prevailing "schizoid mannerisms" of contemporary poetry (two "difficult" poets, John Ashbery and Charles Bernstein, are offered as examples).[3] Wilkinson cites Wieners's "Billie" (1966), a poem whose syntactic chain of signifiers (in contrast, one cannot help noticing, to Wilkinson's paratactic assembly) remains relatively unbroken:

He was as a god,
stepped out of eternal dream

along the boardwalk.
He looked at my girl,
a dream to herself and
that was the end of them.
They disappeared beside the sea
at Revere Beach as
I aint seen them since.
If you find anyone
answering their description
please let me know. I need them
to carry the weight of my life
The old gods are gone. What lives on
in my heart
is their flesh
like a wound,
a tomb, a bomb.[4] (Wieners 1986: 130)

The poem is a version of the "blues" (as in Billie Holliday's "Lady Sings the Blues"), whose distinctive experience is the melancholy of loss. Wieners's poem is not, like Mallarmé's, a poetry of words; it is a "poetry of experience"—a dramatic lyric—in Robert Langbaum's celebrated sense of this term (1963: esp. 38–74). As such—as Wilkinson's title ("Too Close Reading") emphasizes—the poem is meant to be experienced rather than explicated.

What kind of experience?

III. Voices

In "Chamber Attitudes," a fine essay on Wieners's later poetry, Wilkinson cites Wieners's "Understood Disbelief in Paganism, Lies and Heresy," which in this case bears a notable resemblance to Wilkinson's own disjunctive prosody:

Prick any literary dichotomy
sung unrent gibberish from maxim skulls
west Manchester cemetery
recidivist testimony damned
promulgated post-mortem Harry Ghouls
wills pleasant chicanery hulled
in opposition to queer honesty

flying hapless good humours
Morphe erroneous untedious mystery,
non-said mistakes, pure levity
to a method of confused doubt;
lipping erratic contrary indexd.[5] (Wieners 1975: 2)

Wieners's later poetry is often a collage of words; yet, one has to imagine a collage assembled in time rather than space because the question is not how to read the verbal assembly but to imagine what it would be like to hear it:

> This poetry [Wilkinson writes] is composed of chains and clang-associations, and holds to templates; it does not encourage reveries in the reader—rather, it shuts down and cools association, bites back the circumstances, and produces its own speaker, a macaronic first person composed of multiple voices and discourses but simultaneously their virtuoso. Something strange happens to these poems when read aloud, or perhaps when written down, for the compositional priority is impossible to determine: the ghosts of old formal poems may be visible behind accretions, or records of performance may have been tidied up for the page. At whatever point in this to-and-fro, when read by Wieners the poems sound improvised, alive in the voice and almost unimaginably smart, wicked, and poised. (2007: 233)

Recall the concept of "harmolodics": the poem produces not a meaning but a speaker, or rather "a macaronic first person composed of multiple voices"—voices, moreover, united less in choral song than in a *heterophonous* complexity.[6] The reader's task in this event is not hermeneutical but—what, exactly? (Endurance?)

IV. Metastatic Poetics

In an essay on "The Metastases of Poetry" (1994), Wilkinson describes the sort of poetry he admires (and practices) as "a kind of free-standing production process, set up by writers whose erudition is deployed sadistically against the reader" (2007: 152). Wilkinson's preferred site of deployment is not the chair or desk where an exegete tries to make sense of the poem; it is rather the poetry reading—reading as a form of performance art and not the conventional recitation of a text accompanied, say, by the poet's effort "to frame an otherwise highly recalcitrant poetic text, whose recalcitrance is a necessary and specific departure from the language of information and advertising, out of a kindness for the audience or fear of rejection" (153). Wilkinson, for his part, is *against interpretation*: as he confesses, his "reading style has always been confrontational," foregrounding the (sadistically?) *dissentient* temporality of rhythm or cadence rather than that of grammatical and therefore semantic progressions.

Hence Wilkinson's nonconsecutive method of composition, which he calls "metastasis":

> "Metastasis" is a term in rhetoric but my use derives from a brief experience of nursing in a cancer hospice, the way metastatic tumours echo about the body and these nodes define the shape of the body subjectively, through pain. Of course, the location of the primary tumour is outside the poem's realm; the poem develops around the metastatic nodes, and these gestures come to evoke its physical lineaments. The reticence of the primary helps guard against a reductive essentialism in approaching the poem, that it is *about* such-and-such—in fact, there will be a number of extrinsic primaries, too many indeed for amenability. (154)

A metastatic poem thus possesses none of the classical Aristotelian virtues like the subordination of parts to a whole ("the primary tumour is outside the poem's realm"); rather, it is something like a molecular complexity—what Gilles Deleuze and Félix Guattari call a "multiplicity" or variables dispersed in a state of endless variation (1987: 291–98).

Consider, for example, Wilkinson's "Attention and Interpretation":

> A treatise divides between its several heads, yellow
> safe as its green is matter-of-fact, ladies-mantle
> bunched lustrous jar, converges & is close to oceanic—
> No more no more. The earth bread, the millet, maize,
> the repeated cattle voluble as though on cranes' legs,
> where shall these be put? A telephone put its reply
> summarily before a priest calling, stands & clicks
> divining-bones like callipers, adjusted so as to nod
> agreement but in a separate context. It is a protocol
> followed by true, farsighted men. Their fine yellow
> hegemony spreads, in pollen unconstrained but keeping
> bounds lilts toward the future thought to include
> a number of specifics. Take the colourful antidote
> to irony, the sexual check on starvation, shuttles of

> feverish remedies would swerve through roseate water
> plump the little object I which wallowed & withered
> & wallowed again on the lam like an ECHO virus; take
> that ragamuffin seeds & multiplies, cursed to remain
> orphaned ever within its own likenesses—it is clear,
> is it not, is it not, is it not, blue heaven sweats. (2001: 143, 2004: 161)

Perhaps coincidentally, "Attention and Interpretation" is also the name of a Zen-like therapy developed by a physician at the Mayo Clinic to help health-care givers (like Wilkinson) deal with the stress that their occupation frequently produces.[7] The idea, basically, is to practice a form of meditation that concentrates on the mundane particulars of everyday life rather than what goes on in and around one's self. Just guessing, maybe this is the "protocol / followed by true, farsighted men."

But such a guess would be misguided because it makes light of the poet's effort to fend off a reader like me whose philological task is to elucidate the poem, to settle its meaning by way of close reading.[8] Instead, we should take the poem at Wilkinson's word—recall his essay on "metastasis," with its model of tumours that "echo about the body and . . . define the shape of the body subjectively, through pain."

Consider, for example, the color yellow in "Attention and Interpretation"—the way it plays off blue and green (mixing yellow and blue produces green). Yellow is the color of "the earth bread, the millet, maize," echoed by the "fine yellow / hegemony" spread like pollen by "true, farsighted men." The "colourful antidote / to irony" is perhaps off-color, "the sexual check on starvation," but it is merely one example among other "shuttles of / feverish remedies": a pill to be swallowed with "roseate water," except that the anticipated swallowing is displaced by the echo of wallowing, withering, and wallowing again, in which "the little object I" is "on the lam like an ECHO virus"—a virus that, by the way, is metastatic in its distribution throughout the body, "cursed to remain / orphaned ever within its own likenesses" (an Echo virus was originally called an "orphan virus" because it was thought not to be associated with any disease).

V. Poetic Petrifaction

So the poem is not just "schizoid" in its composition, but a mere glossing still misses the force of its energy, which keeps the words of the poem from locking into place. In an essay titled "Repeatable Evanescence," Wilkinson once more emphasizes the priority of "rhythm, rhyme, assonance, consonance" (and doubt-

less *dissonance* as well) in establishing the formal intelligibility—and vitality—
of a lyric poem. The purpose of these features is, in effect, to break down aesthetic distance, namely the habit of readers to stand back and (safely) admire
the poem as if it were a museum piece. To the question, "What is amiss with
admiration?," Wilkinson replies that "the problem lies with the risk of petrifac-
tion" (2007: 24). The paradox of rhythm and other sonic features of a poem is
that they are both "binding and unbinding"; they hold the words of the poem
together even as they set them free from the *stasis* of an objet d'art:

> Successful lyric poetry performs a binding and an unbinding; the poem
> and reader engage in the event as comprising however briefly, however
> tentatively, both a unifying and a freeing. Should binding be perceived
> as excessive, in what might be called a fixation, no event can unfold. . . .
> Lyric fails if incoherent, but fails also if bound into object inertia. (25–26)

Recall the freedom of schizophrenic language from operations of instrumental reason. ("My work life is governed, harried, by instrumental reason," Wilkinson writes in "Mouthing Off" [173].)

"Petrification" is the regulating idea of "Repeatable Evanescence," which
takes up a series of "tombstone" poems by Shakespeare, Herrick, John Berryman, Shelley, Baudelaire, "and a carved stone text designed and sited by Ian
Hamilton Finlay" (27)—a work, says Wilkinson, that, whatever its "integrity
and logic," leaves him "cold" (48). Petrification stills time and makes a poem a
material entity rather than a "temporal performance" (33). Wilkinson thus op-
poses an "aesthetics of the event" (47) to Mallarmé's "aesthetics of the book"
in which, among other things, typography replaces syntax to produce a visual
object (think of the tradition of concrete or visual poetry that takes *Un Coup de
dès* as its progenitor).[9] In a famous passage, Maurice Blanchot, the Aristotle (or
maybe Nietzsche) of *l'écriture*, gives something like a canonical voice to Wilkinson's nemesis:

> My hope lies in the materiality of language, in the fact that words are things,
> too, are a kind of nature—this is given to me, and gives me more than I
> can understand. Just now the reality of words was an obstacle [to predica-
> tion, expression, description, narration]. Now, it is my only chance. A name
> ceases to be the ephemeral passing of nonexistence and becomes a con-
> crete ball, a solid mass of existence [*un massif d'existence*]; language, aban-
> doning the sense, the meaning which was all it wanted to be, becomes
> senseless [*cherche à se faire insensé*]. Everything physical takes precedence:

rhythm, weight, mass, shape, then the paper on which one writes, the trail of ink, the book. Yes, happily language is a thing: it is a written thing, a bit of bark, a sliver of rock, a fragment of clay in which the reality of the earth continues to exist. (1995: 327–28)

It is within and against this conceptual context—the context of literary modernism with its priority of spatial form[10]—that Wilkinson wants to restore the historic temporality (the "repeatable evanescence") of the lyric, which is to say its *orality*, where orality, however, is not to be understood as a form of semantic communication but rather as a kind of imperative that requires the reader to practice something like a *performative* philology (reading the poem aloud, for example). But how, in this event, to read (or hear) Wilkinson? For the paradox is that Wilkinson's harmolodic, metastatic poetry *looks* for all the world like superb examples of modernist innovation, as Wilkinson himself occasionally admits in his essay on "Mouthing Off":

If a poem has a point, for its author it's often at the point of its greatest opacity, since transparency returns the poem to décor, a recital of the known and familiar. (2007: 170)
The *arguments* of my writing are difficult to distinguish from the relationships between words as objects. (173)
I don't think poets have inner lives, their innerness is diverted into the materials they manipulate and combine—or chew over. (173)

Somehow, the lyric is, whatever else it is, neither romantic expressionism nor—paratactic arrangements aside—the objectivist construction of traditional modernism.

Imagine the poem as a kind of echo chamber.

VI. Wilkinson's Lyricism

Let me conclude by trying to engage some parts of Wilkinson's 2015 work, a long, nonlinear, and aggressively recondite poem bearing the enigmatic title *Courses Matter-Woven* (and the equally enigmatic epigraph: "*Unhaunted quite of all but—nothingness?*"). The poem is in ten sections, the first of which reads, or sounds, as follows (forgive the long citation, which you should read aloud):

Pressing Emptiness can't adapt to scurryings not audible:
    stopped down mutely to the clay, stern

Vision buoys up still, through cushions
and through influx, a windsock prolapsed in bronze,
          Peewit calls a dipping dotted course.
          Shining binds the Instrument, analysis
is on a hiding, don't start to think otherwise,
cardboard and tape measures brought for a maquette—
nonetheless a shuffle-deck of feelings slips from cartoon
parameters, each from each, quietly,
          persons run ragged for a stroke
careens just then and there as though it swung against
face-forward, swelling it with what boded ill
beneath the flyover, in the stall underneath straw:
          emaciated palm tree ribs, jutting hips,
simultaneously these expand and organs hang from them,
human brain even, what activity
can be detected in these? Values *en cocotte?* Whispers
also that everyone agrees they ride on the ability to ruffle
edges whether stuck down or gently nodding.
          Ruffled blue tissue awaits its fruit,
ruffled petals spill their scent, awaiting moths' signature
          Until light interrupts,
lathe-cuts a pattern with its shine and slick, figures out
Vestigial Inwardness, till a notched tape pinches a balloon
to get its reading: that inflicts welts:
          invisible respondents pluck and prod,
harrying a Vision of Humanity,
drawing blood that stains oilily the lacquer dogs slither
over, dogs abound and won't be whipped in,—
          rotates in its collar Liberty, sweet Liberty.
At this the seas roar and the votive gulls hung by threads
pitch sickeningly, even as the broken pack
is drawn off by a smell of meat, mills about within its new
restored form.
          In the collar, in the gimbal
spins the human chassis, limbs outstretched and
excruciated in the warp ends of longitude and latitude
picked off from her fingertips, casting
bird coverlets and aeroplanes on predatory mission,

rigged for their remote destinations, brought about.
But she now shrinks within our sights.
But she forms the upside or the downside.
  Birds line up again to test the waters,
sipping at foam.
So she is assembled by numbers.
She kneels in her bracket further bracketed in echoes.
Scurryings and scratches fade, even when the crick throat
gripped in calipers, gasps
across its casing a dashed-off profile moiety while her flip
    upholds a scentless spray of cowslips:
either/or
compounds the Real but what does her cheek press?
  Sung performances fail to
disarray the orange suit or disintegrate the kevlar
before the invisible audience dropping in on this tableau.[11] (2015: n.p.)

Recall Wilkinson's remark about writers like himself "whose erudition is deployed sadistically against the reader." And not just erudition but a series of word combinations that free themselves from the constrictions of context. The poem is a classic of "metastasis": it is not made of substantive predications, nor even (to speak strictly) of words, but of insubordinate "nodes" or "echoes" that one must listen for without having anything like the sense of an ending to guide one through the maze.

Still, the radically open form of the poem is, for someone like me, a constant temptation to interpretation (or at least speculation)—for example, that the poem is, if only periodically, *about* the paradox of "Emptiness" (fertile and lethal by turns) and that we are (perhaps like "the invisible audience dropping in on this tableau") present at matter woven from nothing, as is the woman whose "chassis" is "assembled by numbers," and who "kneels in her bracket further bracketed in echoes."

Bracketed, as if caged.

Or, alternatively, maybe we are the "invisible respondents" who

  pluck and prod,
    harrying a Vision of Humanity,
    drawing blood that stains oilily the lacquer dogs slither
    over.

Emptiness is in any case one of the poem's major "echoes," as in the poem's second section:

> How can nothing
> in itself be cancelled?
> Hold and lock
> gains a firmer grip on emptiness.
> Emptiness condenses in her presence gulping its presence.

Imagine Parmenides reading these lines!
  Or maybe Heraclitus, contemplating these lines from section 3:

> There is no place like no-place blanks,
>   before this null the tulle folds in on itself,
> When Nullity is tremblingly transpired, a contingency felt.

In any event, against all reason, "Emptiness is shaped"—as it is again in the ninth section:

> Under stems of rain the open vowel field quivers
>   rankled Emptiness. Tap its rim.
> The face once applied finds out hollows and would
>   funnel through Vacancies . . . .
> What is this stuff?   I do not bend to pick up,
>   I do not check every pass,
> having been stacked neatly and then staged beside a hedge
> of longitudinal seedlings,
>   a backdrop of wavelets or of harrowed soil.
>   This is Nothing more or less
> composited with no face,
> with no eye to futurity but a set of ploughed cancellations.

Parmenides: "Nothing comes of nothing," to which the poem replies that in the end its paradoxes confine (and silence) us all:

> It is the dead of day. Commotion stills,
>   all companions lie as though comatose from self.
> This is a Special Purpose Vehicle and the future swoops

to re-attach their tongues. Then they settle down,
      millions not yet living
speak with one voice. (section 6)

    Perhaps more impressive, but oddly much to the same point, is that *Courses Matter-Woven* contains a comic aviary of birds—peewits, gulls, starlings, geese, doves, curlews (and, as if by analogy, numerous moths, bees, and a hover-fly). The fifth section tells us that

                    Canada Geese
used to fly in V shapes but directories
darken skies: to one attach the term 'Exemplary'.
        But amongst all individuals
more flocks flock and throngs throng.

Used to fly, but now confinement to cages is the abiding condition (recall the woman enclosed in brackets).

        Heedless of
much-burdened clouds, bird cages rock and toss in waves
as tethered and responding to bungee cords
colour-coded 'pigeon', 'jackdaw', 'woodpecker',

          these cages keep obedient birds
on song, the species sing out of their hymnbooks by name,
mellifluous passages smooth what-needs-must-be.

In section six there are "footprints of birds drying in concrete." In the ninth there is a "swirl of birdsong" and "miscellaneous bird spray," while in the tenth

                A captive wren
falls, sky shatters whirling powder blue smalts,
tongues fitted into slots hinging fluently and laths
        wheel apart.
          What left this residue
crusting on outcrops while night thins
shuttered though it is, shuttered and balked, stuff
shook along the grading trays, sluiced with weak acid—

> car alarms shriek and chatter mockery of crows,
> a new rough edge of doves choking off flow at outlets.
> There is a humming overhead.
> Dust shuffles.
> Tongues cosset corrugated spur bill-&-coo.[12]

And, as if to echo the abiding emptiness:

> Gulls unsupported plunge into negative.

Finally, when "what is called Peewit calls," the poem draws to its ludic conclusion:

> Not having been born sails into its trammels.
> Cloth gets thrown over every cage.

Ironically, "Liberty, sweet Liberty," is the refrain that echoes throughout the poem, as in section 2: "Liberty slashed like a vernal or shocked heath." And near the very end:

> Foreground, centre stage,
> On her turntable a kneeling
> detainee sings and
> calls up the gases. Liberty, oh Liberty
> chimes the one tempor-
> ality, pendant from a leaden plate above her. To be swept
> light, diamond trash.

Hence it is perhaps no wonder that "I" of the poem identifies himself as "a gatekeeper running backwards through gates / and slamming them in your face" (section 2).

So, reader, consider yourself bracketed.

In "Repeatable Evanescence" Wilkinson asks: "How . . . is it possible to distinguish the poem from its interpretation, to resist binding the poem to its interpretation?" (2015: 38). *Courses Matter-Woven* gives us an answer in the form of a practical—*metastatic*—demonstration. It is an evanescent poem that reduces exegesis to the random juxtaposition of citations that echo one another, but which cannot be contextualized or bound coherently together as if some hidden narrative were at work. Rather, the reader is put to flight at every line, as if confined to time's winged chariot.

Which is exactly the point of Wilkinson's poetics: "Densifying and then dissipating, binding and unbinding: such is lyric's main work. Reality needs to be eventuated time and again" (2015: 48).

And so does the reading of his poetry.

PART III

5

Apology for Stuffed Owls

On the Virtues of Bad Poetry

spears of laughter
hiss for a time
then clank across
leaving flakes of rust
—Tom Raworth, "Writing"

I. The Metropolitan Museum of Poetry

Here we will find the Miltonic Sublime, Keatsian Beauty, Mallarmé's *la poésie pure.*

Poetry in its epic, lyric, elegiac modes.

Dreams, visions, strange fits of passion.

Dramatick poesy. Dramatic monologues. Soliloquies ("Am I alone, and unobserved?").

Pindaric odes, Spenserian stanzas, alexandrines, heroic couplets, blank verse, free verse (if not *too* free).

Excuse me. Where would I find "comic poetry"?

(Pause.)

Witty verse, sir?[1]

No, broader, as in "hilarity"

"Hilarity" is usually found in prose, sir.[2] Falstaff. Touchstone. Baudelaire ("On the Essence of Laughter," 1964: 160–71) rightly confines laughter to caricatures on the English stage—Pierrot, for example—and to the stories of E. T. A. Hoffmann. However, we do have an amusing "Sonnet Found in a Deserted Madhouse":

Oh that my soul a marrow-bone might seize!

For the old egg of my desire is broken,

Spilled is the parly white and spilled the yolk, and

As the mild melancholy contents grease

My path the shorn lamb baas like bumblebees.

Time's trashy purse is as a taken token

Or like a thrilling recitation, spoken

By mournful mouths filled full of mirth and cheese.

> (Anonymous, www.sonnets.org/anonymous.html)

You'll find this in the basement, sir. That's where we keep our doggerel. May I recommend, before you descend, Alexander Pope's essay, "Peri Bathous; or, The Art of Sinking in Poetry" (1727)? As every clown knows, comedy requires a repertoire of failures, broken props, exposed backsides.[3]

II. An Aviary of Comic Badness

In 1930 D. B. Wyndham Lewis and Charles Lee published *The Stuffed Owl: An Anthology of Bad Verse*. Here, for example, is a poem by John Armstrong (1709–79), a Scottish physician, addressing what appears to be a disorder of the lower tract:

ADVICE TO THE STOUT

The languid stomach curses even the pure

Delicious fat, and all the race of oil:

For more the oily aliments relax

Its feeble tone; and with the eager lymph

(Fond to incorporate with all its meets)

Coyly they mix, and shun with slippery wiles

The woo'd embrace. The irresolute oil,

So gentle late and blandishing, in floods

Of rancid bile o'erflows: what tumults hence,

What horrors rise, were nauseous to relate.

Choose leaner viands, ye whose jovial make

Too fast the gummy nutriment imbibes. (61)

A neoclassicist would remark upon the failure of decorum: stately form housing (without seeming to notice) a Rabelaisian substance. As the editors of *The Stuffed Owl* explain, the effect is that of a pratfall.

The most obvious and predominating tint [of badness in verse] is bathos: that sudden slip and swoop and slither as down a well-buttered slide, from peaks into the abyss. When some dignified, headline personage, an eminent Academic, a gaitered Divine, an important Actor-Manager, a leading Thinker, a prominent Financier, skids on a scrap of banana-peel in the street and suddenly presents his western façade to the shuddering stars, the impact on the sensations of a thoughtful observer is more tremendous than if the exercise had been performed by a nobody, some urchin, some shabby man of letters, some threadbare saint. (xi)

Which explains why *The Stuffed Owl* is chiefly composed, not of verse by bad poets, but of less-than-inspired efforts of established authors from Dryden to Tennyson, including one of Wordsworth's sonnets:

THE STUFFED OWL
While Anna's peers and early playmates tread,
In freedom, mountain-turf and river's marge;
Or float with music in the festal barge;
Rein the proud steed, or through the dance are led;
Her doom it is to press a weary bed—
Till oft her guardian Angel, to some charge
More urgent called, will stretch his wings at large,
And friends too rarely prop the languid head.
Yet, helped by Genius—untired Comforter,
The presence even of a Stuffed Owl for her
Can cheat the time; sending her fancy out
To ivied castles and to moonlight skies,
Though he can neither stir a plume, nor shout;
Nor veil, with restless film, his staring eyes. (151)

To be sure, "The Stuffed Owl" is an occasional piece (as are many of Wordsworth's poems). So he gives us a real stuffed owl, one that poor Anna cherishes and that stands her in better stead during her illness than did her guardian angel, called away on the Lord's business. Pathos rather than bathos will be the judgment of Wordsworth's champions, but there is no confusing a stuffed owl with a nightingale or skylark, or even with Poe's raven—although it sends Anna aloft to "ivied castles and to moonlit skies." Ordinarily an owl is not a lofty, much less a transcendental, bird; it mainly perches the better to swoop.

Perhaps in pursuit of one of Gertrude Stein's pigeons from "Four Saints in Three Acts" (1972: 605):

Pigeons on the grass alas.

Pigeons, being intrinsically comic, or at all events (like potatoes and carrots) outside the limits of a properly poetic diction, were perhaps Gertrude Stein's favorite bird, notwithstanding James Thurber's protests, registered in one of his *New Yorker* essays, "There Is an Owl in My Room" (1934):

> There is nothing a pigeon can do or be that would make me feel sorry for it or for myself or for the people in the world, just as there is nothing I could do or be that would make a pigeon feel sorry for itself. Even if I plucked his feathers out it would not make him feel sorry for himself and it would not make me feel sorry for myself or for him. But try plucking the quills out of a porcupine or even plucking the fur out of a jackrabbit. There is nothing a pigeon could be, or can be, rather, which could get into my consciousness like a fumbling hand in a bureau drawer and disarrange my mind or pull anything out of it. I bar nothing at all. You could dress up a pigeon in a tiny suit of evening clothes and put a tiny silk hat on his head and a tiny gold-headed cane under his wing and send him walking into my room at night. It would make no impression on me. I would not shout, "Good god almighty, the birds are in charge!" *But you could send an owl into my room, dressed only in the feathers it was born with, and no monkey business, and I would pull the covers over my head and scream.* (my emphasis)

Owls, after all, are birds of prey, as Wallace Stevens reminds us ("The Adequacy of Landscape," 1964: 243):

The little owl flew threw the night,
As if the people in the air
Were frightened, and he frightened them,
By being there.[4]

Leave it to Edward Lear, however, to bring us back to earth—or at least to water (1951: 61):

The Owl and the Pussy-Cat went to sea
    In a beautiful pea-green boat:

They took some honey, and plenty of money
    Wrapped in a five-pound note.
The Owl looked up to the stars above,
    And sang to a small guitar.
"Oh, lovely Pussy, oh, Pussy, my love
    What a beautiful Pussy you are,
        You are,
        You are!
    What a beautiful Pussy you are!"

To the sea, but happily not after the fashion of Icarus, who, reaching for the sublime, suffered a meltdown (Williams, "Landscape with the Fall of Icarus," 1985: 238):

unsignificantly
off the coast
there was
a splash quite unnoticed.

III. Anything Goes

> *Actually*
> *anything does go—but only when*
> *nothing is taken as the basis.*
> —John Cage, "'45' for a Speaker"[5]

Since Aristotle the defense of poetry has meant endowing it with a philosophical seriousness (the task of allegory, for example, was to invest verse with ideas or at all events to make it coherent with the prevailing conceptual schemes by which we try to make sense of things). Recall Friedrich Schlegel (Fr. 238, 1991: 50):

> There is a kind of poetry whose essence lies in the relation between ideal and real, and which therefore, by analogy to philosophical jargon [*der phi-losophischen Kunstsprachen*], should be called transcendental poetry [*Trans-zendentalpoesie*]. It begins as satire in the absolute difference of ideal and real, hovers in between as elegy, and ends as idyll with the absolute iden-tity of the two.

Note that for Schlegel the forms of poetry are defined by their ascent into the idyllic empyrean. *Geistlich* enthusiasm is no doubt their propellant. By contrast,

The shortest
road
from transcendence
to immanence
is
hilarity. (Bernstein, "ms. otis regrets," 2001: 112)

Immanence is made of *haeccesities,* or whatever happens to be at hand ("A poem can be made of anything" (W. Williams, "Kora in Hell," 1970: 70: grocery lists, newspaper clippings). Oblivion awaits the oblivious poet. Recall Wittgenstein (1958: §129): "The aspects of things that are most important for us are hidden because of their simplicity and familiarity. (One is unable to notice something— because it is always before one's eyes.)" It hardly bears repeating that much of modern art and poetry—starting, say, with Marcel Duchamp's *Fountain* (1913) and, before that, Gertrude Stein's *Tender Buttons* (1911)—takes place at ground level. *Tender Buttons,* after all, is famously made of everyday things (objects, food, rooms) that make up Gertrude Stein's life-world, and instead of elevating these things by way of a grand style, she engages them with her own distinctively paratactic comedy:

COLORED HATS
    Colored hats are necessary to show that curls are worn by an addition of blank spaces, this makes the difference between single lines and broad stomachs, the least thing is lightening, the least thing means a little flower and a big delay a big delay that makes more nurses than little women really little women. So clean is a light that nearly all of it shows pearls and little ways. A large hat is tall and me and all custard whole. (1972: 473)

Stein's admirers, in an effort to protect her from decades of ridicule, have been apt to endow her with high seriousness (Ashbery 1957:250, in a review of *Stanzas in Meditation* [1932], compared her work to Henry James's *The Golden Bowl*). In fact the freedom of her ludic juxtapositions constitutes one of the logical conditions that after World War II made so much of innovative art and poetry possible—for example, the music and poetry of John Cage, for whom ambient noises count as art (Cage, "'45' for a Speaker," 1961: 192):

            And what is your purpose
    in writing music? I do not deal
    in purposes; I deal with sounds.

What

      sounds are those? I make

them just as well by sitting quite

still looking for mushrooms.

Or, perhaps more vigorously, the mundane aesthetics of Claes Oldenberg (b. 1929), a sculptor and performance artist who would place ordinary objects (a large replica of an ice cream cone) in incongruous places (atop a skyscraper):

> I am for an art that is political-erotical-mystical, that does something other than sit on its ass in a museum.
>
> I am for an art that grows up not knowing that it is art at all, an art given the chance of having a starting point of zero.
>
> I am for an art that embroils itself with the everyday crap & still comes out on top.
>
> I am for an art that imitates the human, that is comic, if necessary, or violent, or whatever is necessary. (Harrison and Wood, "I Am for an Art," 1993: 728)

To which one might add some lines from the New York poet Frank O'Hara (1930–64), who is remembered for his "I did this, I did that" poems (1995: 400):

> VINCENT
> here I sit in Jager House
> where you got so mad at Gem
> for picking on Bob
>   over a schnitzel
> through the window stains the
> funny air of spring tumbles
> and over the yellow and green
> tables into the brew I sip
> waiting for Roy.

And whose everydayness is marked by occasional tribute to the grotesque body:

> POEM
> Wouldn't it be funny
> if The Finger had designed us
> to shit just once a week?

> all week long we'd get fatter
> and fatter and then on Sunday morning
> while everyone's in church
>> ploop! (351)

Not to mention self-mockery:

> It's so
> original, hydrogenic, anthropomorphic, fiscal, post-anti-aesthetic,
>> bland, unpicturesque and WilliamCarlosWilliamsian!
> it's definitely not 19th Century, it's not even Partisan Review, it's
>> new, it must be vanguard. ("Poem Read at Joan Mitchell's," 265)

Unfortunately there do not seem to be many owls in O'Hara's poetry—his preference seems to have been for larks and parakeets—but those with an interest might profitably consult *The Owls of Central Park* (2011), a volume of photographs, observations, and haikus by Charles F. Kennedy (see Kennedy's website at http://charlesfkennedy.blogspot.com/2009/11/charles-f-kennedy-biography.html).

IV. Digression on the Goose

> *"In dreams begin a lot of bad poetry."*
> —Bernstein, "The Lives of Toll Takers"[6]

In a prolegomena to *The Dunciad* (writing under the guise of Martinus Scriblerus), Pope observed that the muse often tires of flights of genius and so "turneth downward on her wing, and darts like lightening on the *Goose*" (1963: 713). The goose, after all, is, in contrast to the windover, a classically comic bird— Samuel Johnson in his dictionary defined it as "a large waterfowl proverbially noted, I know not why, for foolishness" (http://johnsonsdictionaryonline.com/ ?p=20288). Although, taking for a moment an anthropological view, in Chinese poetry the revered goose sings rather than squawks (www.chinese-poems.com/ lbw1.html). But Robert Southey's "To the Goose" (1848: 119) captures very well the low comedy of English tradition:

> If thou didst feed on western plains of yore
> Or waddle wide with flat and flabby feet

Over some Cambrian mountain's plashy moor,
Or find in farmer's yard a safe retreat
From gipsey thieves and foxes sly and fleet;
If thy grey wills by lawyer guided, trace
Deeds big with ruin to some wretched race,
Or love-sick poet's sonnet, sad and sweet,
Wailing the rigour of some lady fair;
Or if, the drudge of housemaid's daily toil,
Cobwebs and dust thy pinion white besoil,
Departed goose! I neither know nor care.
But this I know, that thou wert very fine,
Seasoned with sage and onions and port wine.

Doubtless one's goose is there to be cooked, even as the word itself is an affront to poetic diction (the more so when "goose" is a verb). Perhaps like most birds it is chiefly poetic in the plural, as in a "gaggle" of geese, although it is doubtful the same can be said of chickens, whose decorum is only preserved when goofy, as in these lines from Jack Prelutsky (1940):

Last night I dreamed of chickens,
There were chickens everywhere,
They were standing on my stomach,
They were nesting in my hair.

V. The Aesthetics of Failure

> *May these put Money in your Purse,*
> *For I assure you, I've read worse.*
> —Alexander Pope, "Couplet"[7]

To gain entry into Plato's republic the ancients aspired to the true, the good, and the beautiful. Comedy's classic theme, by contrast, is freedom from philosophical virtues—a freedom whose spontaneous expression is laughter, as the poet Charles Bernstein reminds us ("G—/," 1986: 208):

i had this liberating thought the other night
imagine that nothing that i write or thought
was good   it was all crummy   and the fact of its

crumminess would somehow free me up from this burden
that i feel to speak to express   to say something
meaningful   because i couldnt   and i an i started
to laugh.[8]

Or, not to put too fine a paratactic point on it, let me cite Tom Raworth's "The Worst Poem" (2003: 49):

electricity flooding the taking place reduction
how hearing letters after not talking
heavy pace flies on screen
food reaction eccentricity
nothing i do spins it off
though the ugliness almost completes the circle.

Here I cannot help recalling Adorno's dialectical pages on the *ugly* in his *Aesthetic Theory* (1997: 45–50), where the ugly is one of modern art's conditions of possibility, which is to say its self-negation, "that antithetical other without which art, according to its own concept, would not exist" (47)—Adorno mentions, among other things, *kitsch*, but perhaps more to the point, the fragment: "The enigma of art works is their fracturedness" (126). Or, again: "Art that makes the highest claim compels itself beyond form as totality and into the fragmentary. The plight of form is most emphatically manifest in the difficulty of bringing temporal art forms to a conclusion. . . . Once having shaken itself free of convention, no artwork was able to end convincingly" (147).

Just so: "The sole path of success that remains open to artworks is also that of their progressive impossibility" (202). As it happens, this is one of the regulating ideas of Lise Le Feuvre's *Failure*, an anthology of writings by modern and contemporary artists on such topics as "Error and Incompetence," which takes up such conceptual paradoxes as intentional badness as in Marcus Verhagen's "There's No Success Like Failure" (2006), and the work of Martin Kippenberger (1953–97), one of whose pieces is entitled *Wittgenstein*, "A lacquered wood construction that looked like a modular piece by Donald Judd but also, and more clearly, like a slightly flimsy closet—it even had a clothes rail. While the title inflated the intellectual span of Judd's work, the sculpture itself effectively likened the artist to a maker of cheap furniture" (Feuvre 2010: 43).

Verhagen notes that "failure . . . was an obsessive concern for Kippenberger,

who cast himself as a failed artist and his work as failed objects and images"
(45), but in so doing, he succeeded as a parodist whose work is a critique of
the art world and the criteria by which a thing (one of Donald Judd's "mini-
malist" constructions—a plywood box, for example) gets counted as art. However, the question of "who's counting?"—art critics, art show curators, artists
themselves?—keeps turning the screw, as Adorno well knew when undertaking
his *Aesthetic Theory* in order to find some way of overcoming the challenge of the
statement with which he begins his great work: "It is self-evident that nothing
concerning art is self-evident anymore, not its inner life, not its relation to the
world, not even its right to exist" (1997: 1); or again, a few pages later: "For no
single select category, not even the aesthetically central concept of the law of
form, names the essence of art and suffices to judge its products" (7). Adorno
was a formalist opposed to "aesthetic nominalism" in which the "aesthetic subject exempts itself of the burden of giving form to contingent material it encounters, despairing of the possibility of undergirding it, and instead shifts the
responsibility for its organization back to the contingent material itself (221)—
as in the unmentionable work of, say, John Cage—

Very frequently no one knows that
contemporary music is or could be
art.
He simply things it was irritating.   **(Clap)**
Irritating one way or another
that is to say
keeping us from ossifying.
It may be objected that from this point
of view anything goes. Actually
anything *does go*—but only when
nothing is taken as its basis. In an utter emptiness
anything can take place. (1961: 160)

Imagine, on this anarchic principle, a poem composed on the model of
Cage's "4' 33'" or perhaps one of Reinhardt's white paintings—in other words a
poem that is simply an empty page, like one of Charles Bernstein's "Great Moments in Taches Blanches" (2013: 98), a poem named after a game of that name
("blank spots" in English) and that comprises simply a numbered list of variations on the uses, literal and otherwise, on the word "blank," with references to

famous aesthetic achievements in blankness like Rauschenberg's erasure of a DeKooning painting, and concluding with a series of parentheses "( )." No. 17 is noteworthy for being a citation of one of Bernstein's most often-used lines, "this section intentionally left blank," and is preceded by, among other things, "a blank stare" (no. 15), and "drawing a blank" (no. 14)—a visual composition that, when realized, is "no longer blank" (96):

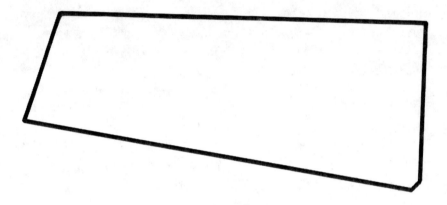

Let this image speak for itself and for the chapter that it brings mercifully to an end.

6

Paratactics ("Pataquerics") of the Ordinary

The Course of the Comic in Charles Bernstein's Poetry

> *I have done everything I possibly could.*
> *I don't know why.*
> *I thought this was kind of typical.*
> *I need people.*
> *I look at the young people.*
> *I'm not going to change my language.*
> —Charles Bernstein, "Sentences"

I. Plain Speaking

In an early essay, "Semblance" (1980), addressing the then-current topic of "the death of the referent," Charles Bernstein took up the question of sentences and what one might do with them:

> "Words elect us. The lamp sits atop the table in the study. The tower is burnt orange." By rotating sentences within a paragraph (a process analogous to jump cutting in film) according to principles generated by and unfolding in the work (rather than in accordance with representational construction patterns) a *perceptual vividness* is intensified for each sentence since the abruptness of the cuts induces a greater desire to savor the tangibility of each sentence before it is lost to the next, determinately other, sentence. (1986: 36–37; my emphasis)

Much of Bernstein's poetry, early and late, is made of isolated or disconnected (and thus *tangible*) sentences, as in "Ballet Russe" (1978):

Every person has feeling.
  It is all the same.
 I will travel.
  I love nature.
 I love motion & dancing.
    I did not understand God. (2000: 75)

Later in the poem, the poet reflects on such sentences:

a lot of what I experience
is a sense of space
& vacant space at that
sort of like a Stanley Kubrick film
sort of a lot of objects floating separately. (77–78)

In Bernstein's "Space and Poetry," space intervenes paratactically in the sentence itself:[1]

space, and poetry
  dying and transforming words, before
          arbitrary, period locked
      with meaning and which
preposterousness. (59)

The idea, basically, is to free sentences (as well as the words within them) from contexts that make them transparent to the point of oblivion. "Rotating sentences," letting them float free, providing each with its own typographic area, gives it a materiality, a "perceptual vividness," that preserves its *sense* from assimilation into a higher order (hypotaxis), where it would simply be an instrument of mediation, a function rather than an utterance that exists, as artworks frequently do, just for itself (Quartermain 1992; Gallego 2012).

Fredric Jameson describes such spacing as "schizophrenic," but interestingly, he remarks, as Bernstein does, on the experience of *vividness* that disjunction produces:

the breakdown of temporality suddenly releases this present of time from all the activities and the intentionalities that might focus it and make it a space of praxis; thereby isolated, that present suddenly engulfs the subject with *undescribable vividness, a materiality of perception properly overwhelming, which effectively dramatizes the power of the material—or better still, the literal—Signifier in isolation.* This present of the world or material signifier comes before the subject with heightened intensity, bearing a mysterious charge of reality, but which one could just as well imagine in the positive terms of euphoria, the high, the intoxicatory or hallucinogenic intensity.[2] (1984: 75).

Bernstein: "Syntax is never what you thought it was; just when you've got it down, it bolts out of the corral into the high chaparral. The job of poetry is not to get syntax back in the corral but to follow its wild journey into the unclaimed" ("How Empty Is My Bread Pudding," 1999: 86–87).

However, what is worth remarking about Bernstein's sentences, whether fragmented or grammatically of a piece, is that they are *plain* rather than "poetical"— in the tradition of William Carlos Williams, for whom poetry should be rooted in the American idiom rather than in the traditional prosodies and closed "poetic diction" of literary history:

> *That which is heard from the lips of those to whom we are talking in our day's-affairs mingles with what we see in the streets and everywhere about us as it mingles also with our imaginations. By this chemistry is fabricated a language of the day which shifts and reveals its meaning as clouds shift and turn in the sky and sometimes send down rain or snow or hail. . . . But of old poets would translate this hidden language into a kind of replica of the speech of the world with certain distinctions of rhyme and meter to show that it was not really that speech. Nowadays the elements of that language are set down as heard and the imagination of the listener and of the poet are left free to mingle in the dance.* (W. Williams 1970: 59; see Bruns 1999: 133–63)

Language "*set down as heard.*" Bernstein would hardly gainsay his connection with Williams—

> *I hate artifice.* All these
> contraptions so many barriers
> against what otherwise can't
> be contested, so much seeming
> sameness in a jello of
> squirms. Poetry scares me. ("Autonomy is Jeopardy," 2000: 307)

—but he would also be inclined to refer us to the American philosopher, Stanley Cavell, foremost champion of the "ordinary language philosophy" of J. L. Austin, as well as of the later writings of Ludwig Wittgenstein, for whom the task of philosophy, like the task of Williams's poet, is attunement to ordinary forms of life, helping us overcome our obliviousness to what is within plain sight.[3]

> One is unable to notice something—because it is before one's eyes."
> (Wittgenstein *1953:* §179)

Or within earshot.

For example, in an early essay, "The Objects of Meaning: Reading Cavell Reading Wittgenstein" (1986: 166–67), Bernstein calls particular attention to Cavell's "use of collage and juxtaposition" rather than consecutive reasoning as a way of thinking: "Whatever answer, whatever authority, he provides comes not from argument but from sounding the words to see what they tell, to make their resonances tangible, and, specifically, with the realization that we literally make the world come into being [or, at all events, to come before us] by giving voice to it."[4]

Sounding the words. Cavell says (1979: xv) that he found Wittgenstein's *Philosophical Investigations* "paradigmatic of philosophy for me, to be a dominating present of the history of philosophy for me. This has meant, as these things will, living with the sounds of it, subjected to the sound." Imagine a poem made entirely of internal echoes:

> None guards the moor where stands
> Receipt of scorn, doting on doddered
> Mill as fool compose compare, come
> Fair padre to your pleated score
> Mind the ducks but not the door
> Autumnal blooms have made us snore. (Bernstein, "Riddle of the Fat
> Faced Man," 1991: 14)

And perhaps not "*sounding* the words" only. In *Philosophical Investigations* Wittgenstein wonders about the experience of letters: "I said that when one reads the spoken words come 'in a special way': but in what way? Isn't this a fiction? Let's look at individual letters and attend to the way the sound of the letter comes. Read the letter A.—We have no idea what to say about it" (1953:

§166). Or, again: "Compare reading with reading words which are printed . . . in capital letters" (§168):

> it got to be very sLOw
> because they say here you wRite this or tHat & after a
> few hundred wORDs i gOt very sPAcey to Continue
> required more attention than I could or was Willing to
> give so i wanted to aSK him what do you mean by it. (Bernstein,
> "eLecTric," 2000: 159)

Or, more radically;

> HH/ ie.s obVrsxr;atjrn dugh seineopeve l iibalfmgmMw
> Er,, me"ius ieigorcyȼjeuvine+pee.)ana/t" ih"n,s
> ortnsihcldseløøpitemoBruce-oOiwvewaa390soanf]++,r"P. (Bernstein,
> "Lift Off," 2000: 176)

I cannot help thinking here of some lines from Williams's *Paterson* (1992: 114):

> Geeze, Doc, I guess it's all right
> but what the hell does it mean?

II. "Insincerity of Form" (Laughter, Groan)

"Lift Off" seems to dispense with everyday speech, but violation of principle, decorum, or expectation (swerving, breaking, going off the edge—what Bernstein has come to call "pataquerics") is equally a distinctive feature of Bernstein's anarchic poetics.[5]

For example, in an essay on "Comedy and the Poetics of Political Form" (1988), Bernstein describes his own work in terms of what he calls "the insincerity of form" (1992: 220):

> Such poetic play does open into a neat opposition of high irony and wet
> lyric expressiveness but, in contrast, collapses into a more destabilizing
> field of pathos, the ludicrous, schtick, sarcasm; a multidimensional tex-
> tual field that is congenitally unable to maintain an evenness of surface
> tension or a flatness of affect, where linguistic shards of histrionic inap-

propriateness pierce the momentary calm of an obscure twist of phrase, before cantoring into the next available trope; less a shield than a probe.[6]

Consider, by way of example, these lines from "The Lives of Toll Takers":

> [*a mixture is worth a thousand one-line serves*].
> Nei
>   ther
>   speaking the unspeakable nor saying
>   the
>   unsayable
>   (though no doubt slurring
>   the unslurrable): never only
>   dedef
>   ining, always rec
>   onstricting (libidinal
>   flow just another
>   word for loose
>   st
>   ools). There was an old lady who lived in a
>   zoo,
>   she had so many admirers
>   she didn't know what to rue. (1994: 11)

What is more "ludicrous" (or hilarious) than rotations of bad puns? (But aren't all good puns bad—or vice versa?) And what sinks the "poetical" more completely than a joke about defecation? Moreover, "insincerity of form" means never knowing what comes next—except perhaps

> Debris—I thought as little of that
> as of your hand covering it, as if
> to do good was somehow foolproof.
> You arrive in discrete packets over years
> and the composite is neither immaculate
> nor contingent. Seek love and the winter
> falls in our faceless naming, a
> bill sent for recollection, attaining
> a lift from a lisp. Go ahead:

live on the tongue just as you clam
up in company. ("in between," 2001: 15)

Comic wordplay—"linguistic shards of histrionic inappropriateness"—is, Bernstein would say, his shtick:

Not that I mean to startle just
unsettle. The settlers pitched their tents
into foreign ground. All ground is
foreign ground when you get to know
it was well as I do. Well I wouldn't agree.
No agreement like egregious
refusal to hypostatize a suspension.
Suspension bridges like so many
drummers at bat, swatting flies
in the hot Carolina sun. No, son, it
wasn't like that—we only learned we
had to be proud not what's worth taking
pride in. ("Locks without Doors," 1994: 51)

One can and, indeed, should think of Bernstein as a stand-up comic.[7] In "Optimism and Critical Excess" (1992: 178) he writes:

Whoa! Nellybell! Just a minute there. Not so fast.
  I wonder if humor isn't getting lost in the shuffle, getting the short end of the rib, so to speak, playing backseat driver to anecdote on a slow trip on the backroads late at night in the dense, unforgiving fog.
  Against seriousness as such. Humor breaks the "high poetic" frame, showcases conflict.

Here is how Bernstein figures himself in "Solidarity Is the Name We Give to What We Cannot Hold" (1999: 33):

I am a serial poet, a paratactic poet, a
disjunctive poet, a discombobulating poet,
a montage poet, a collage poet, a hypertextual
poet, a nonlinear poet, an abstract poet,
a nonrepresentational poet, a process poet,

a polydiscourse poet, a conceptual poet.
I am a vernacular poet, a talk poet, a dialect
poet, a heteroglossic poet, a slang poet, a
demotic poet, a punning poet, a comic poet.

A canonical piece in this regard would be "The Manufacture of Negative Experience" (2001: 28–33), which Bernstein describes as follows: "It's a constellation or array, or then again maybe a charm bracelet. One of my obsessions has been to include—fully and faithfully (or is it faithlessly, I always get those confused)—a set of Henny Youngman style jokes within a poem" (2011: 247).[8]

My bread has some nerve. No
sooner does it come out of the oven
than I have to slap it for being
so fresh. (2001: 28)
"When I say 'no' I mean
maybe, probably not, what's
the matter with you?, do I
make myself clear? is anybody
out there?, do you serve a
no-doze with your lecture? (30)
Is the Pope Jewish? Is that perfume
coming from your backside? Are
you happy with your lot in life? Are
you vastly overpaid for your services?
Is there anything that scumbag jerkoff
has done for you lately? (33)

What these lines have in common with most nightclub stand-up gigs is that, after each punch line, one might hear a drum riff in place of laughter, which is part of the comic routine, since most jokes (and poems) are comic chiefly in virtue of their failure.

Or consider "Invention Follies" (2011: 35): "Of course, the risk of invention is that your invention fails; it usually fails, since most art produces failure, no matter its successes. The risk of not inventing is to succeed—at little or nothing. So these are the poles: it can be admirable to succeed at nothing (I have made a point of it) just as it can be illuminating to fail at innovation."

Of course, as Bernstein says (2013: 6–7): "So much depends on what you mean by failure, what you want from success, and what you imagine poems do. Insofar as a poem is successful, it fails to fail, but, in failing to fail, it also succeeds at failing. That's a lose-lose scenario (which in the alchemy of poetry we imagine as win-win)."

Or, again (10): "*Tumble, sunder, fake, fail.* These are not only my subjects but also practice (makes imperfect). Does the poem allow its error to lead? rupture? collapse? rapture?"

> I've always loved Sally Silvers' work:
> especially her early work where
> she does stuff with movement that's extremely awkward
> a kind of awk-
> wardness that you don't
> associate with dancers.
> I always wanted
> to do something like that
> with poetry
> to make poetry almost
> painfully
> clumsy, clumpsy. ("Talk to Me," 2013: 14)

III. New York Intermezzo

> —*For the purpose*
> *Of your request I'm including this*
> *Sentence about the influence of John*
> *Ashbery.*
> "The Influence of Kinship Patterns upon Perception of an
> Ambiguous Stimulus"[9]

It is worth noting as an aside that there is little that resembles Bernstein's comic poetry in *The Oxford Book of Comic Verse*, where the humor depends as much on lilting metrics and witty rhyme schemes as it does on the subject matter, as in this poem by Richard Tipping (Gross 1994: 473):

> When you're feeling kind of bonkers—
> Got a screw loose, round the bend;
> When you're crazed, berserk, gone potty,
> Don't know really from pretend;
> You'll be flipped out, strung, bananas,

Off your rocker, flicking nuts,
'Cause the booby-hatch and loony bin
Can't dot the "I" on all our buts.

Closer to home might be a poem by David Lehman:

One Size Fits All: A Critical Essay
Though
Already
Perhaps
However.
On one level,
Among other things,
With
And with.
In a similar vein
To be sure:
Make no mistake.
Nary a trace . . .
Which is to say,
In fictional terms,
For reasons that are never made clear,
Not without meaning,
Though (as is far from unusual)
Perhaps too late. (470)

The virtue of this poem, such as it is, is its satirical edge—it is composed of the stock words and phrases of a book review (the very sort of thing Bernstein would ridicule). Interestingly, Lehman is the author of a fine book on the New York School of poets, and he makes the point that many of Charles Bernstein's poems, "which are very funny, make me think he's a New York School poet in disguise" (1999: 370).

Consider John Ashbery, for example:

Suppose this poem were about you—would *you*
put in things I've carefully left out:
descriptions of pain, and sex, and how shiftily
people behave toward each other? Naw, that's
all in some book it seems. For you

I've saved the description of chicken sandwiches,
and the glass eye that stares at me in amazement
from the bronze mantel, and will never be appeased. ("The Problem of
Anxiety," 2007: 185)

Ashbery's shtick is rather more rabbit-out-of-the-hat ("For you / I've saved the
description of chicken sandwiches") than Bernstein's rapid-fire one-liners, but it
is comic all the same, not the least because of its plain-speaking. A bit broader
(or lower) is "Laughing Gravy":

The crisis has just passed.
Uh-oh, here it comes again,
Looking for someone to blame itself on, you, I . . .
All these people coming in . . .
The last time we necked
I noticed this lobe on your ear.
Please, tell me we may begin.
All the wolves in the wolf factory paused
At noon, for a moment of silence. (209)

Ashbery is a master of throw-away incongruities—*laughing gravy* might pass
for a metaphysical conceit (disparate ideas yoked by violence together) were it
not for the poet's deadpan delivery—as if wolves at work in a wolf factory were
an ordinary form of life.

To which Bernstein might reply: All very well, but the point to remember
is that there is no one such thing as "the comic": "Anything that departs from
the sincere or serious enters into the comic, but the comic is anything but a
unitary phenomenon, and the range of comic attitudes goes from the good hu-
mored to the vicious, from clubby endorsement of the existing world to total
rejection of all existing human communities" (1992: 227). The comedian, after
all, is the classic outsider.

IV. Exposure and Bewilderment

In "The Practice of Poetics" Bernstein writes:

To practice poetics is to acknowledge the inevitability of metaphor, the lin-
guisticality of perception, the boundedness of thought, the passion of ideas,
the beauty of error; the chains of logic, the possibilities of intuition, and

the uncanny delight of chance. In contrast to the syllogistic rationality of expository writing, poetry is situational, shifts with the winds, courts contradiction, feeds on inconsistency. (1992: 73)

Poetry is *situational*—finds its *metier* in "the beauty of error" and "the uncanny delight of chance." But Bernstein's later poetry raises this question: How does comic poetry as "The Art and Practice of the Ordinary" respond to (or live with) a darker species of chance, namely *catastrophe*?

Stanley Cavell, philosopher of the ordinary or of how it is with us in everyday life, figures our relation to the world—and to the people in it—not as a matter of cognition (which is how much of Western philosophy since Descartes and Kant has pictured it: namely in terms of a disengaged punctual ego exercising conceptual control over its experience) but as a condition of *exposure*:

> I do not picture my everyday knowledge of others as confined but as exposed. It is exposed, I would like to say, not to possibilities but to actualities, to history. . . . The worst has befallen, befalls every day. It has merely, so far as I know, not befallen me. Tragedy figures my exposure to history as my exposure to fortune or fate; comedy as my exposure to accident or luck. Each will have its way of figuring this as my exposure to nature; meaning in the end, human nature. As if the subjection to history *is* human nature. (1979: 432)

And exposure or subjection to history frequently begins (and often continues) in disbelief, as in Bernstein's "It's 8:23 in New York," composed on September 11, 2001:

> It was hard not to feel like it was a movie, and one with an unbelievable plot at that. All the airports closed; the Pentagon bombed; four commercial jets highjacked on suicide missions. The bridge was overflowing with people streaming out of Manhattan, a line as wide as the bridge and as long as Manhattan itself. If you looked out to the left, there was a big plume of smoke over downtown Manhattan. You couldn't see that the Towers were not there . . .
> Uncanny is the word.
> What I can't describe is the reality; the panic; the horror . . . .
> This could not have happened. This hasn't happened.

This is happening.[10] ("It's 8:23 in New York," 2006: 17–19; see Lagapa 2012: 172–91)

No doubt "insincerity of form" seems inappropriate in such cases, since in such cases we are no longer on the same ground with the *ordinary*, which heretofore had been "considered as possible material to be transmuted, sputtered, turned topsy turvy or tipsy flopsy" (2011: 248). Imagine catastrophe as a "form of life." In "Aftershock," Bernstein remarks: "Things I do everyday like make airplane reservations on the phone are now fraught with an unwanted emotional turbulence" (2006: 24). Ironically, Bernstein had once figured poetry "as turbulent thought": "At least that's what I want from it, what I want to say about it just here, just now (and maybe not in some other context). It leaves you unsettled, unresolved—leaves you knowing less than you did when you started" (1999: 42–43). Turbulent thought remains for Bernstein a poetic signature:

> *Hold tight!*
> 　　　　The rink round the
> posing is closed for retrofitting.
> 　　　　　　Refurbishment
> is just around the hospital coroner:
> 　　　　　　　If bald
> bring hat; if not, ignore this sentence but be sure
> to complete the rest of the lines in the poem
> before going on to part four. ("Choo Choo Ch'Boogie," 2006: 44–45)

As do fragments and aphorisms, as in "In Parts":

> we call it minimalism but it's nearly rococo. (96)
> the artist articulates the differences society obliterates. (99)
> a series is a sequence without origin or destination simply occurrence. (99)
> or else the syntax inside the nouns touch. (103)

And "charting the verbal environment of the moment" (1992: 177) is likewise Bernstein's continuing task, although in the aftermath of catastrophe there is a notable shift to a different, more ambiguous register. "What I am trying to do in my writing is to produce an experience of language as social material" (2011: 179), but in *Girly Man* "social" becomes something more stringent and even

philosophical, as in "War Stories," a series of aphorisms on the complexity—
indeed, the internal contradictions—of war:

> War is the first resort of scoundrels.
> War is the legitimate right of the powerless to resist the violence of the
> powerful. (2006: 149)
> War is the slow death of idealism.
> War is realpolitik for the old and unmitigated realism for the young.
> War is pragmatism with an inhuman face.
> War is for the state what despair is for the person. (150)
> War is the opiate of the politicians.
> War is to compromise what morbidity is to mortality. (151)
> War is not won but survived.
> War is two wrongs obliterating right.
> War is the abandonment of reason in the name of principle.
> War is sacrifice for an ideal. (152)

And then there is "The Ballad of the Girly Man," a thumbnose at Arnold Schwarzenegger:[11]

> The truth is hidden in a veil of tears
> The scabs of the mourners grow thick with fear
>
> Thugs from hell have taken freedom's store
> The rich get richer, the poor die quicker
> & the only god that sanctions that
> Is no god at all but rhetorical crap
>
> So be a girly man
> & take a gurly stand
> Sing a gurly song. (179)

"Gurly" is a Scottish term meaning "rough" or "boisterous," like the aphorisms
in "Self-Help," which offer sarcastic, even angry, responses to the bloody lunacy
of twenty-first-century life:

> War toll tops 100,000.—Get your mind off it, switch to reality TV . . .
> Subway floods and late for audition.—Start being author of your own
> performance. Take a walk. (171)

Hurricane crushes house.—You never seemed so resilient.
Brother-in-law completes second-year in coma.—He seems so much more
relaxed than he used to. (172)

Retirement savings lost on Enron and WorldCom.—They almost rhyme.
Oil spill kills seals.—The workings of the Lord are inscrutable.
Global warming swamps land masses.—Learn to accept change. (173)

V. The Black Sun of Comedy

Recall Cavell: "The worst has befallen, befalls every day. It has merely, so far as
I know, not befallen me."[12]

Oh, lucky man!

A long tradition credits comedy as a force that distances us from the maladies
of experience—and even, as in Samuel Beckett's work, from "the worst": distances us, but only, as the philosopher Simon Critchley says, until "the laughter
dies away," leaving us exposed to "the black sun of depression at the heart of the
comic" (2007: 50; see also Critchley on Beckett, 2004: 184–88). In this respect
Bernstein's volume of poems *Recalculating* brings us up against the "black sun"
of comedy, whose formal turbulence is shadowed on nearly all of its pages by
the death (in 2008) of his daughter, Emma.

> Each day I know less than the day before. People say that you learn some-
> thing from such experiences; but I don't want that knowledge and for me
> there are no fruits to these experiences, only ashes. I can't and don't want
> to "heal"; perhaps, though, go on in the full force of my dysabilities, co-
> existing with a brokenness that cannot be accommodated, *in the dark.* ("Re-
> calculating," 2013: 174)

What distinguishes *Recalculating*, among other things, is the way memory
rather than comedy provides the unifying energy of the collection. Many of the
poems (*pace* W. C. Williams) are translations, renditions, and remembrances
of a number of European poets whose work often registers the suffering of
loss—Celan's famous Holocaust poem, "Totnauberg" (Bernstein 2013: 80), for
example, and one of Apollinaire's First World War poems, "Ombre" (38). It is
not that Bernstein has abandoned his ludic turbulence. *Recalculating* opens, for
example, with "Autopsychographia (*after Fernando Pessoa*)"—

Poets are fakers
Whose faking is so real
They even fake the pain
They truly feel
And for those of us so well read
Those read pains feel O, so swell
No the poets' double header
But the not of the neither
And so the wheels go whack
Ensnaring our logical part
In the train wreck
Called the human heart. (3)

—and includes (of all things) a *'zaum* poem after the Russian futurist, Velimir Khlebnikov, "Incantation by Laughter":

We laugh with our laughter
loke lafter un loafer
sloaf lafker int leffer
lopp laprer und loofer
loopse laper ung lasler
pleap loper ech lipler
bloop uffer unk oddurk
flop flaffer ep flubber
fult lickles eng tlickers
ac laushing ag lauffing uk
luffing up luppling uc
lippling gas prickling
urp laughter oop laughing
oop laughing urp laughter. (94)

But more generally Bernstein's one-liners are registers of pain—"I've grown so accustomed to the dark that I can hardly imagine anything more than shadows" (177)—and the volume concludes with an elegy ("Before You Go") that simply trails off into typographic oblivion:

Thoughts inanimate, stumbled, spare, before you go.
Folded memories, tinctured with despair, before you go.

Two lakes inside a jar, before you go.
Flame illumines fitful lie, before you go.
Furtive then morrow, nevering now, before you go . . .
Coriander & lace, stickly grace, before you go.
Englobing trace, fading quakes, before you go.
Suspended deanimationation, recalcitrant fright, before you g
Everything so goddamn slow, before you
Take me now, I'm feelin' low, before yo
Just let me unhitch this tow, before y
One more stitch still to sew, before
Calculus hidden deep in snow, befor
Can't hear, don't say, befo
Lie still, who sings this song, bef
A token, a throw, a truculent pen, be
Don't know much, but that I do, b
Two lane blacktop, undulating light. (184–85)

In the end, one has little heart to say anything more: "*We are most familiar with our estrangement; it is our home ground*" (126). As if one had suffered exile to a new "form of life" in which one can no longer be at home. But perhaps this is the fate of the comedian—did I not call him "the classic outsider"?

PART IV

7

On the Words of the *Wake*

(and What to Do with Them)

Discourse is thus the experience of something absolutely foreign . . . a traumatism of astonishment.
—Emmanuel Levinas, *Totality and Infinity*

. . . in the Nichtian glossery which purveys aprioric roots for apostriorious tongues this is nat language in any sinse of the world . . . .
—James Joyce, *Finnegans Wake*

I once imagined Joyce's *Finnegans Wake* as a realization (of sorts) of Flaubert's "book about nothing, a book dependent on nothing external, which would be held together by the strength of its style, . . . a book which would have almost no subject, or at least the subject would be almost invisible" (Flaubert 1953: 127–28; Bruns 1974: 142). To put such a book into play, writing would have to free language from its traditional functions of mediation: designation, predication, narration, expressions of feeling, or (in short) forms of world making whose aim is to make things, including ourselves, intelligible. One way to accomplish this emancipation would be to materialize language, treating words as things—for example, as typographical arrangements of letters on a page, as in Stéphane Mallarmé's *Un Coup de dés* (1895):

C'ÉTAIT   LE NOMBRE
            issu stellair

                                    EXISTÂT-IL
                        autrement qu'hallucination éparse

d'agonie

                            COMMENÇÂT-IL ET -IL

sourdant que nié et clos quand apparu

enfin

par quelque profusion répandue

en rareté

SE CHIFFRÂT-IL

évidence de la somme pour peu

qu'une

ILLUMINÂT-IL

CE SERAIT   LE HASARD

pire

non

dadvantage ni moins

indifféremment mois autant

Choit

la plume

rhythmique suspens du sinistre

s'ensevelir

aux   écumes

originelles

naguères d'où sursauta son délire jusqu'à

une cime

flétrie

par la neutralité identique du

gouffre.

In writing such as this, Mallarmé explains, "we avoid narrative [*on évite le récit*]," so that the purely formal pattern of words—its "withdrawals, prolongations, evasions [*retraits, prolongements, fuites*]"—will result in "a musical score for anyone wishing to read aloud. The difference in typefaces [*caractères d'imprimerie*] between the predominant motif, a secondary one, and those adjoining dictates its importance to the oral utterance [*l'émission orale*], and its range, average, up and down the page, will mark whether the intonation rises or falls" (Mallarmé 1965b: 210–11).

Mallarmé's real achievement, however, was not just to musicalize language but also, and more importantly, to incorporate the white space of the printed page into the formal structure of the poem, leading one to imagine a "cenographic" poem, whose surface would resemble the "white paintings" of artists like Kazimir Malevich and Robert Rauschenberg.[1] This would mean taking literally Mallarmé's famous remark: "My work was created only by elimination. . . . Destruction was my Beatrice."[2]

By contrast, Joyce's method, in much of *Ulysses* and all of *Finnegans Wake* is that of the rhetorical figure of *amplificatio*, the heaping up of words and things—a process that (as in the work of Rabelais) always threatens to break any frame that could contain, among other unities, a narrative.[3] Recall the famous inventory of "The house of O'Shea or O'Shame, *Quivapieno*, known as the Haunted Inkbottle":

> For this was a stinksome inkenstink, quite puzzonal to the wrottel. Smatterafact, Angles aftanon browsing there thought not Edam reeked more rare. My wud! The warped flooring of the lair and soundconducting walls thereof, to say nothing of the uprights and imposts, were persianly literatured with burst loveletters, telltale stories, stickyback snaps, doubtful eggshells, bouchers, flints, borers, puffers, amygdaloid almonds, rindless raisins, alphybettyformed verbage, vivlical viasses, ompiter dictas, visus umbique, ahems and ahahs, imeffible tries at speech unasyllabled, you owe mes, eyoldhyms, fluefoul smut, fallen lucifers, vestas which had served, showered ornaments, borrowed brogues, reversible jackets, blackeye lenses, family jars, falsehair shirts, Godforsaken scapulars, neverworn breeches, cutthroat ties, counterfeit franks, best intentions, curried notes, upset latten tintacks, unused mill and stumpling stones, twisted quills, painful digests, magnifying wineglasses, solid objects cast at goblins, once current puns, quashed quotatoes, messes of mottage, unquestionable tissue papers, seedy ejaculations, limerick damns, crocodile tears, spilt ink, blasphematory spits, stale shestnuts. (Joyce 1958: 183.6–25)

And so on, through dozens of additional items. Here we have Shem, "writing the mystery of himsel in furniture" (184.9–10); or, in the same stroke, Joyce ("a mixer and wordpainter" [87.13]) on what the *Wake* is made of, namely a virtually infinite dictionary of multiple and heterogeneous words (or should one say "syllables"?) struggling to inhabit simultaneously a finite set of lexical, syntactical, and typographical spaces. (Like many modernist works, the *Wake* is perhaps never so intelligible as when it is self-reflexive.) Any given word of the *Wake* is, potentially and in fact more often than not, the incarnation (and obliteration) of many others: a glossolalia of "alphybettyformed verbage"—phonemes, portmanteaus, puns, and plagiarisms ("The last word in stolentelling" [424.35]).[4]

However, one should nevertheless emphasize that, in contrast to Flaubert's or Mallarmé's dream of a pure work of art, there is rarely some sense that cannot be made of any fragment of Joyce's text ("So you need hardly spell me how every word will be bound to carry three score and ten toptypsical readings" [20.13–15]). There are no secrets, nothing behind or beneath the handiwork; everything is out in the open, riding the surface of serial letter- and wordplay:

> Ullhodturdenweirmudgaardgringnirurdrmolnirfenrirlukkilokkilbaug-
> imandodrrerinsurkrinmgeernrackinarockar! Thor's for yo!
> —The hundredlettered name again, last word of perfect language.
> (424.2–24)

Of course, the difficulty with such a surplus of floating signifiers is that it threatens to break down the classical unity of text and context—

> Was that in the air about when something is to be said for it or is it someone imparticular who will somewherise for the whole anyhow? (602.7–9)

—which is why there once (not so long ago, and even now) seemed to be nothing for it but to go beyond a mere reading or exegesis of the text. On this view, the *Wake* turns us against hermeneutics onto the path of structural analysis, where the end of reading is no longer to determine the meaning of anything but rather to lay open to view the deep structure or mode of production that makes meaning, or whatever, possible.[5] So meanings, proliferating uncontainably, are replaced by tacit rules and systematic relations. Accordingly, mainline semioticians like Umberto Eco figure *Finnegans Wake* as "a model of the global semantic system," or (alternatively) as "a metaphor for the process of unlimited semiosis" (1985: 252),[6] which simply means that the *Wake* is *structured* as a language, never mind the consequences. Its surface formations are protean and self-interfering like the surfaces of everything else—the body, history, what you will—but structuralist analysis can penetrate these formations to grasp an underlying rationality. The spirit of such analysis is captured by Louis Althusser's famous idea that "the religious myth of reading" begins to dissipate with Marx's discovery that "the truth of history cannot be read in its manifest discourse, because the text of history is not a text in which a voice (the Logos) speaks, but the inaudible and illegible notation of the effect of a structure of structures" (1970: 17). Something other, something deeper than the legibility of meaning is at work. Call it, after Marx (or Nietzsche), power, or, after Freud, desire. Questions of power and desire are technological rather than hermeneutical. "The question posed by desire," say Gilles Deleuze and Félix Guattari (1983: 109), "is not 'What does it mean?' but '*How does it work?*'" "Desire," they say, "makes its entry with the general collapse of the question, 'What does it mean?' No one has been able to pose the problem of language except to the extent that linguists have first eliminated meaning; and the greatest force of language was only discovered once a *work* was viewed as a machine, producing certain effects, amenable to a certain use." Thus, Jean-Michel Rabaté (1984: 81): "The metaphor of the machine describes not only the [*Wake's*] theoretical functioning, but also the labour which constructed it. . . . Joyce means to capture in his machine all the fluxes he diverts, the flux of language and the flux of history."[7] So from the standpoint of technology one may put it that *Finnegans Wake* operates like a graphic dispenser whose "manifest discourse" displaces the question of reading from fiction to function, from meaning to desire, from consciousness to the unconscious, from faith to suspicion, from ideology ("the religious myth of reading") to critique.

Speaking of machines, it is true that the *Wake* has its share of them—

> Now, while I am not out now to be taken up as unintentionally recommending the Silkebjorg tyrondynamon machine for the more economical helixtrolysis of these amboadipates until I can find space to look into it myself a little more closely first I shall go on with my decisions after having shown to you in good time how both products of our social stomach (the excellent Dr Burroman, I noticed by the way from his emended food theory, has been carefully digesting the very wholesome criticism I helped him to in my princeps edition which is all so munch to the cud) are mutuearly polarised the incompatabililiy of any delusional acting as ambivalent to the fixation of his pivotism. (Joyce 1958: 163–64.29–39)

The "fixation of his pivotism"—no doubt "indicating that the words which follow may be taken in any order desired" (121.12–13).

The unkillable idea, of course, is that *Finnegans Wake* works like a dream and the reading of it requires something like a psychoanalytic model of analysis in which a latent content is constructed by recombining into coherence the surface debris of the manifest discourse (after all, "by writing thithaways end to end and turning, turning and end to end hithaways writing and with lines of litters slittering up and louds of latters slettering down . . . where in the waste is the wisdom?" [114.16–20]; see Norris 1974: 4–11, and 1976: 98–118). A unique example of this sort of thing would be John Bishop's *Joyce's Book of the Dark*, which is perhaps uncontroversial in its critical observations and results but worth close attention for the way it incorporates the *Wake*'s words into its own discursive arrangements:

> "How many of its readers realize" (112.1–2 [*really* realize]) "that [it] is not out to dizzledazzle with a graith uncouthrement of . . . the lapins and the grigs"? (112.36–133.3). The referentially secure languages of "Latin" and "Greek," of course, are helpful to the reading of the *Wake*, but less so than a knowledge of "*lapins*" (Fr. "rabbits") and "grigs" (Eng. "crickets"), which leap all over the place, "runnind hare and dart" (285.4), rather like the nocturnal thought of the "quhare sort of mahan" whose sleeps at the *Wake* (16.1). Because it is an "imitation of a dream-state" and not rationally discursive thought, *Finnegans Wake* is written in "coneyfarm leppers" (257.5–6) ["coneys" = "rabbits"]), and not "cuneiform letters," or, again, in "some little laughings and some less of cheeks" (125.15) [and even less "Latin" and "Greek"]. What it really requires of its reader is the ability to pursue "distant connections" (169.4–5) and, in doing so, to leap all over the place. "*Read your Pantojoke*" (71.17–18 [and not the "Pentateuch"]). (1986: 307)

Bishop likes to say things like "all the printed letters and words in *Finnegans Wake* are mere 'vehicles' leading to hidden meanings and letters that are nowhere explicitly evident to a reader's literate consciousness" (310), but all he means by this is that we should not try to read the thing the way we would a proposition or a narrative. The method of reading that Bishop counsels (and practices) is not formally different from the sort proposed by Clive Hart—what Hart calls "motifs" (1962: 4) are "long chains of association" for Bishop, and the idea is simply to trace these chains (or rather reconstruct them) by piecemeal attention to the combinatory power of the text's elementary particles. Since this power is considerably in excess of what normally fits under the category of linguistic competence, reading has a lot to do. The question is: What motivates such reading? Bishop says:

> Any reading wishing to "read the Evening World," as opposed to "the dully expressed" [the *Daily Express*], must therefore learn to "stotter from the latter" with the hero of the *Wake*, by slipping from the literal surface of the

text and becoming a freethinker of sorts. Making "infrarational" and "freely masoned" connections is ultimately more important to an understanding of the *Wake*'s "slipping beauty" (477.23 ["sleeping beauty"]) than making literate distinctions, which is the business of the "day's reason." (1986: 307)

Becoming "a freethinker of sorts" seems to me to capture something essential: one has to let go of the imperative, or foundations, of explanation and become something like a participant or collaborator, a "cryptoconchoidsiphonostomata in his exprussians" (Joyce 1958: 135.16).

In the essay "Within the Microcosm of 'The Talking Cure,'" Julia Kristeva writes about ways in which an analyst might come to terms with his or her patient's "borderline discourse" (1983: 40). A "borderline discourse" is one that exhibits "the maniacal eroticization of speech, as if the patient were clinging to [language], gulping it down, sucking on it, delighting in all the aspects of an oral eroticization and a narcissistic safety belt which this kind of non-communicative, exhibitionistic, and fortifying use of speech entails. The analyst notices a tendency to play with signifiers, which are not always, not only, or sometimes not at all cultural acquisitions" (42). How to read such corporealized speech?

The analyst often feels called upon, especially in the beginning of the cure, to "*construct relations*," to take up bits of discursive chaos in order to indicate their relations (temporal, causal, etc.), or even simply to repeat these bits of discourse, thereby already ordering these chaotic themes. This kind of logical, even associative, task could give the impression that we work at constructing repression. More precisely, and in light of the "sign" function and its perturbations, these constructions serve to give the speech act a *signification* (for a subject—the analyst, the patient). This repetition or reordering by means of an interpretation that builds connections does not serve to reconstruct either a real or an imaginary biography. Instead, it reestablishes plus and minus signs and, subsequently, logical sequences and thus the very capacities of speech to enunciate exterior referential realities. (45–46)

So, on this model, one might imagine a reader of the *Wake* trying to repair Joyce's text, making it readable by rewriting it according to the model of the proposition, the narrative, or the signifying system (for example the interplay of metaphor and metonymy). In fact, it is this sort of repair work that makes up the bulk of Joyce criticism, and perhaps not just of Joyce's difficult texts but of much of avant-garde writing of the last century and a half. One recalls Jürgen Habermas's idea that the task of criticism is to translate the innovative forms of contemporary art and literature into "normal language" in order to integrate them into the problem-solving life-worlds of "communicative praxis" (1990: 204–10).[8]

> We feel unspeechably thoughtless over it all here in Gizzygazelle Tark's bimboowood so pleasekindly communicake with the original sinse we are only yearning as yet how to burgeon. (Joyce 1958: 238.35–239.2)

But Kristeva goes on to speak of "condensed interpretations" that bear a more "erotic" relationship to the borderline text; instead of trying to repair the text, condensed interpretation embraces it in all of its materiality: "It separates non-sense from the restrictions of meaning and colludes with the manic or narcissistic manipulation of the signifier in the borderline patient" (1983: 46). On this model, *Joyce's Book of the Dark*, as a work of "constructive interpretation," mostly reinvents the wheel; as a species of "condensed interpretation," however, it is a *tour de force*. For it is not so much that Bishop tries to penetrate the materiality of Joyce's language as the other way around: the language of the *Wake* is internalized—it would not be too much to say "cannibalized"—in Bishop's "reading" of it (1986: 219):

> "It is a mere mienerism of this vague of visibilities," "for inkstands" (608.1 [Fr., *vague*, "empty"], 173.34), that terms like "shade," "tar," "coal," "pitch," "soot," and "ink" should everywhere occlude words that are otherwise "basically English" (116.26). With intricate particularity, these "blackartful terms" (121.27) enable the *Wake* to adopt its own peculiar "dressy black modern style" (55.14–15), a "blackhand" "sootable" to the portraiture of "*a blackseer*" who is given to envisioning only vast "blackshape[s] and lots of "pitchers." (495.2; *L*, III, 147; 340.13; 608.29; 233.1, 438.13, 531.15, 587.14, 598.21)

To be sure, this sentence is explanatory after a fashion, but Bishop's obsessive quotation from Joyce's text is more erotic than analytic; it does not try to rebuild the text within a framework of signification but "colludes" with its "manic or narcissistic manipulation of the signifier."

Naturally we want to know the point of such a reading, what justifies it, what its cash value is; but the point of such a reading is just to free itself from the norms of Habermas's "communicative praxis." This means entering into the region of *délire*, which is Jean-Jacques Lecercle's word for

> a form of discourse which questions our most common conceptions of *language* (whether expressed by linguists or by philosophers), where the old philosophical question of the emergence of sense out of *nonsense* receives a new formulation, where the material side of language, its origin in the human body and *desire*, are no longer eclipsed by its abstract aspect (as an instrument of communication or expression). Language, nonsense, desire: *délire* accounts for the relations among these three terms. (1985: 6)

Délire describes the opposition between the dictionary and the scream. It occurs "at the frontier between two languages [as] the embodiment of the contradiction between them." On the one hand, there is the language of signification, that is, language as the functioning of *langue*, language as system and rule, "an instrument of control, mastered by a regulating subject"—"not to be broched by punns and reedles" (Joyce 1958: 239.34–35); but on the other hand there is language in its material density or thickness:

> unsystematic, a series of noises, private to individual speakers, not meant to promote communication, and therefore self-contradictory, "impossible" like all "private languages." It is an integral part of the speaker's body, an outward expression of its drives. It imposes itself on the individual, controlling the "subject": it is not the transparent medium that the instrumentalist describes, nor the means of consensus that the conventionalist conceives, it is, to misquote a philosophical phrase, a (material) process without a subject. (Lecercle 1985: 44–45)

If we think of the *Wake* as belonging to the region of *délire*—"It darkles (tinct, tint) all this our funnaminal world" (Joyce 1958: 244.13)—it becomes evident that the reading of the *Wake* can no longer be conceived as an analytical process, that is, a process of getting down to something *essential* (a "deep structure," among other things). In *Finnegans Wake*, as a work of *délire*, the essential has been displaced by the *excessive*. The *Wake* is a product, not of *langue*, but of *lalangue*, which is Jacques Lacan's word for that which *langue* excludes (1972: 126–27). *Lalangue* is language in its heterogeneity, its materiality, its irreducibility to the functions of reason, its uncontainability within any framework, system, or limit—

Imagine the twelve deaferended dumbbawls of the whowl abovebeugled to
be the continuation through regeneration of the urutteration of the word
in pregross. (Joyce 1958: 284.18–22)

Lalangue is, psychoanalytically, that which must be repressed if consciousness is to form. In Lacan's lingo, it is that which blasphemes the Name of the
Father and plays havoc with the Symbolic Order ("The Function and Field
of Speech," 1977a: 67–68). Not surprisingly, for Lacan *lalangue* is distinctively
Joycean: it is not a concept but an "infelicity" of speech, a stuttering or even a
kind of sound or visual poetry:

Lukkedoerendunandurraskewdylooshoofermoyportertooryzooysphal
nabortansporthaokansakroidverjkapakkapuk. (Joyce 1958: 257.27–28)

Lacan writes (1977a: ix): "I shall speak of Joyce, who has preoccupied me much
this year, only to say that he is the simplest consequence of a refusal—such a
mental refusal!—of a psychoanalysis, which, as a result, his work illustrates." If
psychoanalysis—that is, a normalizing "constructive interpretation" of borderline discourses—aims at the reinsertion of a text into the order of signification,
Finnegans Wake is a refusal of such analysis. Instead, it invites erotic transgression into "condensed interpretation" where the reader lets go into "the madness of words" (68–70).

(Imagine erotic philology—forgive the tautology—as a critical method.)

A compelling example of such transgression is John Cage's series, "*Muoyce*
(Writing through *Finnegans Wake*)," the most intriguing of which is the fifth
(1983: 174):

rufthandlingconsummation tinyRuddyNew-
permienting *hi* himself then pass ahs c
e *i* u flundered e w myself s ct making
Hummels ct life's She to east time the
thesion br is thosen *southsates* i over
thg the he an ndby fluther's sees e as
brown ou a as m her i i *The Vortex*glad.[9]

A slightly different example is to be found in Jacques Derrida's *Glas* (1974), a
collage of texts that forms an erotic triangle with Hegel and Jean Genet (Derrida 1986: 1):

what, after all, of the remain(s), today, for us, here, now, of a Hegel?

For us, here, now: from now on that is what one will not have been able to think without him.

For us, here, now: these words are citations, already, always, we will have learned that from him.

Who, him?

His name is so strange. From the eagle it draws imperial or historic power. Those who still pronounce his name like the French (there are some) are ludicrous only up to a certain point: the restitution (semantically infallible for those who have read him a little—but only a little) of magisterial coldness and imperturbable seriousness, the eagle caught in ice and frost, glass and gel.

Let the emblanched [*emblémi*] philosopher be so congealed.

Who, him? The lead or gold, white or black eagle has not signed the text of *savoir absolu*, absolute knowledge. Even less has the red eagle. Besides, whether *Sa* is a text, has given rise to a text, whether it has been written or has written, caused writing, let writing come about is not yet known.

Sa from now on will be the siglum of savoir absolu. And IC, let's note this already since the two staffs represent each other, the Immaculate Conception. A properly singular tachygraphy: it is not first going to dislocate, as could be thought, a code, i.e., what we depend [table] on too much. But perhaps, much later and more slowly this time, to exhibit its borders

Whether it lets itself be assigned [*enseigner*], signed, ensigned is not yet known. Perhaps there is an incompatibility (rather than a dialectical contradiction) between the teaching and the signature, a schoolmaster and a signer. Perhaps, in any case, even when they let themselves be thought and signed, these two operations cannot overlap each other [*se recouper*].

Its/His [*Sa*] signature, as thought of the remain(s), will envelop this corpus, but no doubt will not be contained therein.

This is—a legend.

Not a fable: a legend. Not a novel, not a family romance since that concerns Hegel's family, but a legend.

remain(s) to be thought: it, (ça) does not accentuate itself here now but will already have been put to the test on the other side. Sense must conform, more or less, to the calculi of what the engraver terms a counterproof

The legend does not pretend to afford a reading of Hegel's whole corpus, texts, and plans [*desseins*], just of two figures. More precisely, of two figures in the act of effacing themselves: two passages.

"what remained of a Rembrandt torn into small, very regular squares and rammed down the shithole" is divided in two.

As the remain(s) [*reste*].

Two unequal columns, they say distyle [*disent-ils*], each of which — envelop(e)(s) or sheath(es), incalculably reverses, turns inside out, replaces, remarks, overlaps [*recoupe*] the other.

The incalculable of *what remained* calculates itself, elaborates all the *coups* [strokes, blows, etc.], twists or scaffolds them in silence, you would wear yourself out even faster by counting them. Each little square is delimited, each column rises with an impassive self-sufficiency, and yet the element of contagion, the infinite circulation of general equivalence relates each sentence, each stump of writing (for example, "*je m'éc . . .*") to each other, within each column and from one column to the other of *what remained* infinitely calculable.

Almost.

Of the remain(s), after all, there are, always, overlapping each other, two functions.

The first assures, guards, assimilates, interiorizes, idealizes, relieves the fall [*chute*] into the monument. There the fall maintains, embalms, and mummifies itself, monumemorizes and names itself—falls (to the tomb(stone)) [*tombe*]. Therefore, but as a fall, it erects itself there.

I

Derrida thought of this as "a sort of *Wake*," although the page arguably owes its look to Mallarmé's typographical experiments.[10]

Glas is the sort of thing Habermas had in mind (1990: 205) when he complained against "the *aestheticizing of language, which is purchased with the twofold denial of the proper senses of normal and poetic discourse*," namely, argumentation and world disclosure. Imagine Hegel's *Geistesgeschichte* as a storm of words:

The June snows was flocking in thuckflues on the *hegelstomes*, millipedes of it and myriopoods, and a lugly whizzling tournedos, the Boraborayellers, bloahblasting tegolhuts up to tetties and ruching sleets off the coppeehouses, playing ragnowrock rignewreck, with an irritant, penetrant, siphonopterous spuk. (Joyce 1958: 416–17.32–37; my italics)

Lecercle aligns *délire* with the private languages of psychosis. However, one might want to supplement or open up this line of thinking a little further by replacing *délire* with Bakhtin's notion of the *carnivalesque*, which is a historicized rather than psychic (much less systematized) category of discourse (1984: 122–37; and LaCapra 1983: 291–324, on Bakhtin's "carnivalesque"). That is, the carnivalesque brings *délire* into the open—onto the street, into a non-Habermasian public sphere as an anarchic region of "communicative praxis" from which nothing is excluded, nothing is forbidden (except rules, limits, censors, or any form of repression). Whereas, following Habermas, we must (at least in school) conceive the public sphere philosophically as a space opened up by argument; the carnivalesque describes a public realm shaped by the sort of "maniacal eroticization of speech" that produced *Finnegans Wake*. In fact, we may think of the *Wake* as opening up just such a public space (into which, for example, all commentary on the *Wake* must enter, even if this means leaving the gated community of the university, whose task is to ensure the legitimacy of critical readings). Bakhtin redistributes the distinction between surface and deep structure horizontally along a social axis instead of vertically according to ascending planes of logical integration. In this respect he may be said to have freed language from the residual transcendentalism of the various semiotic, psychoanalytic, and paleo-/poststructuralisms ("Sink deep or touch not the Cartesian spring!" (Joyce 1958: 301.24–25). Thus, unitary language and the heteroglossia are social rather than grammatical categories of speech; they compete with one another along the same plane for control of the public eye and ear (Bakhtin 1981: 270). They are like the celebrated distinction that Derrida (1989: 103–4) once drew between Husserlian and Joycean language:

> Both try to grasp a pure historicity. To do this, Husserl proposes to render language as transparent as possible, univocal, limited to that which, by being transmittable or able to be placed in tradition, thereby constitutes the only condition of a possible historicity. . . . The other great paradigm would be the Joyce of *Finnegans Wake*. He repeats and mobilizes and babelizes the (asymptotic) totality of the equivocal, he makes this his theme and his operation, *he tries to outcrop, with the greatest possible synchrony, at great speed, the greatest power of meanings buried in each syllabic fragment*, subjecting each atom of writing to fission in order to overload the unconscious with the whole memory of man: mythologies, religion, philosophies, sciences, psychoanalyses, literatures. This generalized equivocality of writing does

not translate one language into another on the basis of common nuclei of meaning. (my emphasis)

A "pure historicity" would be one that is completely outside the ideality of settled meanings, an open, turbulent, unstructured temporality of colliding or intersecting surfaces—a *complexity* that cannot be mapped by an external geometer (cannot be thought). Only by entering into this historicity, however, can the ideality of meaning be actualized (that is, as actually saying something); only when this happens does historicity become intelligible. Husserlian language enters this space seeking total intelligibility; it tries to bring historicity under control, shaping it in its own image according to a geometry of pure relations or the pure forms of meaning: "As in pure (what bunkum!) essenesse" (Joyce 1958: 608.4). Joycean language, by contrast, lets itself go, turns itself loose in this continuum, and disrupts it with its heterogeneity and irreducibility to univocal sense. In "Two Words for Joyce" Derrida (thinking of the following passage from the *Wake*) asks us to imagine "the possibility of writing several languages at once" (1984: 149):

Go to, let us extol Azrael with our harks, by our brews, on our jambses, in his gaits. To Mezouzalem with the Delphilim, didits, dinkun's dud? Yip! Yup! Yarrah! And let Nek Nekulon extol Mak Makal and let him say unto him: Immi ammi Semmi. And shall not Babel be with Lebab? And he war. And he shall open his mouth and answer: I hear, O Ismael, how they laud is only as my loud is one. (Joyce 1958: 258.7–13)

Thus, on the one hand, we may imagine a social order superintended by a universal grammar into whose forms everything can be translated and understood by everyone no matter what time or place; and, on the other, we have a world in which *all* words are alien, where no one is saying anything except "incelleneteutoslavzendlatinsoundscript" (219.16–17).

Bakhtin's linguistics (or antilinguistics) sees these two languages in ideological conflict. He describes an "elastic environment of other, alien words" that must be brought to order—dominated, if only momentarily, at some point or intersection—if anyone is to make sense to anyone else (see Stewart 1983: 276). There is, at all events, no making sense anywhere except within this environment; that is, there is no setting up an alternative semantic space where sentences cohere transparently around a logical form. Husserl-like, Bakhtin imagines a word trying to connect up with its object, but, Joyce-like, he imagines this taking place in a sort of radio-culture of intersecting (interfering) idioms:

> Indeed, any concrete discourse (utterance) finds the object at which it was directed already as it were overlain with qualifications, open to dispute, charged with value, already enveloped in an obscuring mist—or, on the contrary, by the "light" of alien words that have already been spoken about it. It is entangled, shot through with shared thoughts, points of view, alien value judgments and accents. The word, directed toward its object, enters a dialogically-agitated and tension-filled environment of alien complex inter-relationships, merges with some, recoils from others, intersects with yet a third group: and all this may crucially shape discourse, may leave a trace in all its semantic layers. (1981: 276)

The idea is that intentions are never alone with their objects in the purely logical (or monological) space of the proposition; they belong to the "dialogized heteroglossia," proliferating within a circle, whose center is everywhere and whose circumference is indeterminate. Imagine the proposition, not as a sealed off logical form (*s* is *p*), but as porous and exposed not only inwardly toward psychic otherness and figural difference but externally toward an alien sociality, a "Tower of Babel mixing of languages" (278). Husserl-like, Bakhtin picks out the relation of word and thing; Joyce-like, he situates this relation within a Babel of "alien words":

> On all its various routes toward the object, in all its directions, the word encounters an alien word and cannot help encountering it in a living, tension-filled interaction. Only the mythical Adam, who approached a virginal and as yet verbally unqualified world with the first word, could really have escaped from start to finish this dialogic inter-orientation with the alien word that occurs in the object. Concrete historical human discourse does not have this privilege: it can deviate from such inter-orientation only on a conditional basis and only to a certain degree. (279)

So there is no pure, pre-Babel relation of word and thing: "The word is born in a dialogue as a living rejoinder within it; the word is shaped in dialogic interaction with an alien word that is already in the object. A word forms a concept of its own object in a dialogic way" (279). Or, to put it plainly, each of us, when we speak, is more *Wakean* than we realize because we build our sentences out of words with a history, indeed several histories and multiple etymologies, words that come down to us in traditions of multifarious voices filled with the echoes of conflicting and crumbling contexts. One's discourse floats in a Sargasso Sea of usage. Bakhtin's idea, in any case, is that one's voice is always intersected by other voices, laced with other intentions, other worlds, as if one were always caught up in an urban noise of marketplace and fish market, street corner and train station, pub and union hall, where everyone is talking at once and nobody is anyone who does not sound like someone else ("wi'that bizar tongue in your tolkshap" [Joyce 1958: 499.21]).[11]

I cannot forbear inserting here some lines from the Brazilian poet Haroldo de Campos's Joycean *Galaxias, 1963–1976*, a Portuguese verbivocovisual construction made of words like "horáriodiáriosemanáriomensárioanuário." It begins as follows:

> *e começo aqui e meço aqui ese começo e recomeço e remeço e arremesso*
> *e aqui me meço quando se vive sob a espécie da viagem o que importa*
> *não é a viagem mas o começo da por isso meço por isso começo escrever*
> *mil páginas escrever milumapáginas para acabar com a escritura para*
> *começar com a escritura para acabarcomeçar com a escritura por isso*
> *recomeço por issue arremeço por isso teço escrever sobre escrever é*
> *o future do escrever sobrescrevo sobrescravo em milumanoites miluma-*
> *páginas ou uma página em uma noite que é o mesmo noites e páginas.*[12]
> (1984: 1)

About which Haroldo de Campos writes (1977: 58): "The text is defined as a 'flux of signs,' without punctuation marks or capital letters, flowing uninterruptedly across the page, as a *galactic* expansion. Each page, by itself, makes a 'concretion,' or autonomously coalescing body, interchangeable with any other page for reading purposes. . . . [The book] constitutes a search for 'language in its materiality,' without 'beginningmiddleend.'"

Let me conclude by following Walter Benjamin's principle of citation as a good in itself. Here is a long quotation from the *Wake's* final pages (1958: 614.27–615.10).

Our wholemole millwheeling vicociclometer, a tetradomational gazebocroticon (the "Mamma Lujah" known to every schoolboy scandaler, be he Matty, Marky, Lukey or John-a-Donk), autokinatonetically preprovided with a clappercoupling smeltingworks exprogressive process, (for the farmer, his son and their homely codes, known as eggburst, eggblend, eggburial and hatch-as-hatch can) receives through a portal veil the dialytically separated elements of precedent decomposition for the verypetpurpose of subsequent recombination so that the heroticisms, catastrophes and eccentricities transmitted by ancient legacy of the past, type by tope, letter from litter, word at ward, with sendence of sundance, since the days of Plooney and Columcellas when Giancinta, Pervenche and Margaret swayed over the all-too-ghoulishly and illyrical and innumatic in our mutter nation, all, anastomosically assimilated and preteridentified paraidiotically, in fact, the sameold gamebold adomic structure of our Finnius the old One, as highly charged with electrons as hophazards can effective it, may be there for you, Cockalooraloooraloomenos, when cup, platter and pot come piping hot, as sure as herself pits hen to paper and there's scriblings scrawled on eggs.

Another machine! A "tetradomational gazebocroticon . . . autokinatonetically preprovided with a clappercoupling smeltingworks exprogressive process." A self-operating mythopoeic system that works like a hen producing what eventually becomes an Easter egg. It is a messy digestive process—the gazebocroticon "receives through a portal veil the dialytically separated elements of precedent decomposition for the verypetpurpose of subsequent recombination"—that gives us our heroic history: "The heroticisms, catastrophes and eccentricities transmitted by ancient legacy of the past, type by tope, letter from litter, word at ward, with sendence of sundance," all of it as if by genius "anastomosically assimilated and preteridentified paraidiotically" as the story of the eternally recurring HCE ("Finnius the old One").

The question is whether one's experience of the citation profits from the gloss or whether it were better (if only for erotic philological reasons) to let Joyce's words do what they do best:

> We seem to understand apad vellumtomes muniment, Arans Duhkha, among hoseshoes, cheriotiers and etceterogenious bargainboutbarrows, ofver and umnder, since, evenif or although, in double preposition as in triple conjunction, how the mudden research in the topaia that was Mankaylands has gone to prove from the picalava present in the maramara melma that while a successive generation has been in the deep deep deeps of Deepereras. Buried hearts. Rest here. (595.21–29)

"Rest here." Just so.

8

What's in a Mirror?

James Joyce's Phenomenology of Misperception

*The mirror's ghost lies outside my body, and by the same token my
own body's "invisibility" can invest the other bodies that I see. Hence
my body can assume segments derived from the body of another, just as
my substance passes into them; man is the mirror for man. The mirror
itself is the instrument of a universal magic that changes things into a
spectacle, spectacles into things, myself into another, and another into
myself.*

—Maurice Merleau-Ponty, "Eye and Mind"

I. Joyce's Mirrors

Let me begin with Hugh Kenner's remark (1956: 123) that the basic unit of
Joyce's fiction is the encounter, as in the *Dubliners* story of that name. The
most famous of these events is perhaps Stephen's "vision" of the birdlike girl
on Sandymount strand, who is not likely to be the creature he thinks he sees—
remember at this point in his life Stephen's eyes are rather more mirrors than
windows of his soul (1964: 171). And then there is the meeting of Stephen and
Bloom in *Ulysses*: "Silent, each contemplating the other in both mirrors of the
reciprocal flesh of theirhisnothis fellowfaces" (1986: 577), where the two are
exact reversals of one another, as in a chiasmus, the symmetry of hydrophobe
and hydrophile being only one of the more comic of their mirror-connections.[1]

Je est un autre, as Rimbaud famously remarked (1962: 5).

I would like to propose that Joycean encounters are philosophically interesting because, in various literal or figurative ways, they are made of mirrors
that defeat logical notions of identity (I = I) in favor of the idea that relations
of self and image are unstable, excessive, and work more often like interrup-

tions than connections: "I am another now, and yet the same" (1986: 10), says Stephen. But (at least in *Ulysses*) it is his otherness that he mainly experiences because his alterity keeps multiplying its forms, often before his very own eyes. I want to consider Joyce's mirrors in some detail and to argue that Joycean encounters are phenomenological rather than empirical, which means that what is seen, heard, or experienced is conditioned by the variable and conflicted intentional horizons within which these encounters take place.[2] Recently such scenes have lent themselves to psychoanalytic interpretations or to inquiries into the nature of the image in Joyce's fiction.[3] My approach here is to follow instead the idea that perception is frequently overdetermined, uncontainable within logical rules of identity. That is, experience is always experience of contexts, of which there is always more than one, so there is always more to people and things than meets the eye. In just this wise, Joyce's fiction shows how experience is multiple, heterogeneous, overdetermined, and fraught with layers and fractures that overlap and interrupt one another in ways that it takes (readers like us) a lifetime of close reading and exertions of memory to sort out. In this respect we are very like Joyce's characters.[4]

Let me proceed (again) by following Benjamin's method of glossed citations (1999: 290). For example, I have always been drawn to those wonderful moments of self-encounter, as when, in "The Dead," Gabriel Conroy is captured like a snapshot by his mirror: "As he passed the way of the cheval-glass he caught sight of himself in full-length, his broad, well-filled shirt-front, the face whose expression always puzzled him when he saw it in a mirror and his glimmering gilt-rimmed eyeglasses" (Joyce 1996 218). The brute function of a mirror is to produce a likeness of what passes before it. But what plainly interests Joyce is the way mirrors do not quite do this—the way they do not produce empirical mirror-images but, on the contrary, register multiple forms of difference: alienation, alternative or multiple identities, and unauthorized or embellished versions of dubious originals, but also sometimes the fulfillment of a happy wish.[5] All the while (as I will try to explain) mirrors somehow tell the truth, in the sense that some sense of fitness, sometimes desirable but more often otherwise, rules the encounter. In any event, it is the nature of mirrors to catch us off guard, as if filling in blanks we usually keep empty. Imagine always being puzzled by the look on your face, as if you were the author of an expression that, try as you may, you will never understand (or forget). What is unsettling is not the shock, but the failure, or maybe fear, of recognition. The mirror tells a tale of self-estrangement, where you encounter yourself as someone else, a lost or failed self, or at least someone sufficiently different so as to interrupt your self-possession. (The mirror as a medium of disillusionment is surely a major trope of naturalism.) So Gabriel had expected to see himself reflected in his wife's eyes, or in her memory, but instead he found Michael Furey there, a more memorable and romantic version of what he had hoped himself to be. Hence the famous tailspin:

> Gabriel felt humiliated by the failure of his irony and by the evocation of this figure from the dead, a boy in the gasworks. While he had been full of memories of their secret life together, full of tenderness and joy and desire, she had been comparing him in her mind with another. A shameful consciousness of his own person assailed him. He saw himself as a ludicrous figure, acting as a pennyboy for his aunts, a nervous, well-meaning sentimentalist, orating to vulgarians and idealizing his own clownish lusts, the pitiable fatuous fellow he had caught a glimpse of in the mirror. (1996: 219–20)

II. Phantasmagoria

On the question of mirrors, Joyce may be compared with W. B. Yeats, who said that "man is nothing till he is wedded to an image" (1966: 749), where image means not self-image but image or incarnation of another. A mirror in this case would produce, not a likeness of the original, but what the original secretly embodies: namely, an identity or meaning from another world. Yeats's idea is that by itself the individual is a mere cipher, but when doubled via history, a poet with Yeatsian eyes would be able to construe a true image and likeness— Maud Gonne as Helen, and vice versa: or think of the girl in "Among School Children" who reincarnates the young Maud, with the poet's memory invoking a Quattrocentro portrait of a noblewoman in the bargain—"mirror on mirror mirroring all the show" (Hugh Kenner's favorite Yeatsian line). Imagine a mirror that does not tell you what you look like but what you are (or were), or what you would be if only the times were in joint. In the Yeatsian system doubling is metaphorical rather than mimetic because it involves the turning of someone into something otherwise: a mask, an antiself, an archetype. So much of Joyce's work (as Kenner thought) seems a parody of Yeats's theory, for example as laid out in Yeats's "Ego Dominus Tuus." Hence Bloom as Odysseus. But perhaps it is also an exploration of Yeats's metaphysics from within the frame of everyday life, where counterparts run the gamut back and forth from the mythical-ironic to the trivial-heroic.

Possibly, we can put this more simply. In Joyce doubling turns an image into something saturated with meanings, both divergent and convergent, as when Mulligan thrusts a mirror at Stephen in "Telemachus":

> —Look at yourself, he said, you dreadful bard.
>
> Stephen bent forward and peered at the mirror held out to him, cleft by the crooked crack, hair on end. As he and others see me. Who chose this face for me? The dogsbody rid of vermin. . . .
>
> Laughing again, he brought the mirror away from Stephen's peering eyes.
>
> —The rage of Caliban at not seeing his face in the mirror, he said. If Wilde were only alive to see you. (1986: 6)

You may recall from the *Portrait* what Stephen did after writing his first poem:

> After this the letters L. D. S. were written at the foot of the page and, having hidden the book, he went into his mother's bedroom and gazed at his face for a long time in the mirror of her dressingtable. (1966: 71)

We are not told (here) how the young Stephen saw himself, but we can imagine what he is looking for—a change, at least, and even if possible, a recognition (anyway it is an early self-portrait of the artist).[6] For the crucial question in each moment of self-regard is not how accurately the original has been reproduced but how to *take* the image that appears in its place, especially when there are, as in Stephen's case, a surplus of heterogeneous images, none of which is implausible on the face of it. Indeed, no one in Joyce's fiction is more haunted by images than Stephen. For example, of the image in the cracked looking glass he says: "As he and others see me." The mirror does not give back an image of *Stephen's* Stephen but only Mulligan's Stephen, or someone else's ("if Wilde were only alive to see you"—and what would Wilde have seen? Possibly the lugubrious picture of an unwashed Dorian Gray for whom, however, there is no unafflicted counterpart). Stephen will spend the whole day encountering other people's Stephen. He has worked hard not to take his likeness from his surroundings but (Dubliner that he is) to little avail: "Who chose this face for me?" he wonders, as if his likeness were only something to be put on like a mask, an unfitting image, the resemblance of a merely local progenitor. What Stephen wants to do is to produce, mirrorlike, his own image—in fact this is just the expression that turns up in "Proteus," the episode that gives a detailed montage of Stephen's self-experience. Musing, appropriately, upon disguises, he says: "I'll show you my likeness one day" (1986: 36). But what would Stephen, one day, look like?[7] He is, as he says, "looking for something lost in a past life" (38). Someone irrecoverable, as if the real question were whether there is any longer in Stephen any original that he could show us. Aging overlays or displaces originals, as any of us can testify. One could take this to be the point of Mulligan's remark about the rage of Caliban. It is not, in Stephen's case, that the mirror is merely empty but only that the face he sees is never really his, so that self-regard more often than not is an experience of mistaken, received, or anyhow unwanted identity—and a corresponding experience of dispossession (the theme of "Telemachus"). "Who chose this face for me?" he wonders, and soon a line in "Proteus" answers: "You're your father's son" (36), meaning in particular that eyes and voices twin Simon and Stephen both in their own eyes and in those of others. Consubstantial father and son, indeed (32). It is not that Stephen is not what he appears to be; it is that he seems powerless to be anything else: call him a creature of saturated phenomena (a Proteus *malgre lui*). His desire is for self-creation—"The Father Who is Himself his own Son" (171)—but instead, or so far, he is mostly someone in whom other people trace resemblances of their own imagining, as, famously, does Bloom:

> Still, supposing he had his father's gift, as he more than suspected, it opened up new vistas in his mind, such as Lady Fingall's Irish industries concert on the preceding Monday, and aristocracy in general.
>
> Exquisite variations he [Stephen] was now describing on an air *Youth here has an end* by Jans Pieter Sweelinck, a Dutchman of Amsterdam where the frows come from. . . .
>
> A phenomenally beautiful tenor voice like that, the rarest of boons, which Bloom appreciated at the very first note he got out, could easily, if properly handled by some recognized authority on voice production . . . command its own price where baritones were ten a penny and procure its fortunate possessor in the near future an *entrée* into fashionable houses in the best residential quarters, of financial magnates in a large way of business and titled people. (541–42)

Just so, as Molly says, Poldy "ought to get a leather medal with a putty rim for all the plans he invents" (630).

So perhaps we should speak of Stephen's missing resemblance and the corresponding gap in their own lives that people use their experience of him to fill ("I suppose hes 20 or more Im not too old for him," muses Molly [637]). The question is: What is the status of this *other* who always takes the place of what one wants to see when one looks at oneself? What I want to say is that in Joyce's fiction the mirror produces, not an image of what it sees, but a mis-resemblance that nevertheless attaches itself to the original (or stands in for it, possibly re-forming it) more or less permanently—call it a near-self, someone else whom you were or someone you could have been (in yours or someone's eyes) or someone you might yet become or perhaps are destined but will fail to be ("so grieved he also in no less measure for young Stephen for that he lived riotously with those wastrels and murdered his goods with whores" [320]). The possibilities are endless, but inevitably an original of some (now indeterminate) sort is obscured, scattered, or merely replaced. It is hard not to think here of Keats's notion of the poet as someone who has no character, who is nothing in himself and is not to be found in any of his creations; rather, he is a pure power of impersonation, someone able to turn himself into anyone at all. Imagine the Keatsian poet turned into Joycean mirror-play, with Stephen as a poet no longer in control of his impersonations: someone himself turned into a mirror ("See me as others see me").

Of course, Joyce does not mind reversing this state of affairs as often as he stages it. Recall Stephen's face-to-face experience of the unfortunate Cyril Sargent, which is only one of multiple events in which others are Stephen's mirror: "Like him was I, these sloping shoulders, this gracelessness. My childhood bends beside me. Too far for me to lay a hand there once or lightly. Mine is far and his secret as our eyes. Secrets, silent, stony sit in dark places of both our hearts: secrets weary of their tyranny: tyrants willing to be dethroned" (24). Better perhaps to say that at different moments Joyce's different characters experience mirrors differently. Recall the end of "Nausicaa," when sated Bloom (after having—another mirror-event—just picked up Stephen's abandoned scribblings—see "Proteus") writes in the sand:

> Mr Bloom with his stick vexed the thick sand at his foot. Write a message for her. Might remain. What?
>
> I.
>
> Some flatfoot tramp on it in the morning. Useless. Washed away. Tide comes here a pool near her foot. Bend, see my face there, dark mirror, breathe on it, stirs. All these rocks with lines and scars and letters . . .
>
> AM. A.
>
> No room. Let it go.
>
> Mr Bloom effaced the letters with his slow boot. Hopeless thing sand. (312)

The word "efface" is interesting in this context. Instead of a missing resemblance—Caliban's rage and so on—we have a resemblance that is deleted: Bloom, seeing his face mirrored in a tidepool, breathes on it, and then wipes away his self-predication ("AM. A."). This shutting down or repression of self-regard (if that is what it is) is, of course, perfectly understandable, given Bloom's self-weariness, which mirrors Stephen's in the usual inverted way, since Stephen's desire for self-regard is deflected by a series of defacements, whereas Bloom desires invisibility—"see not be seen" (218)—and perhaps even nonidentity—"no one is anything," says the modern Nobodaddy (135). Effacement and defacement are, let us say, twin forms of alienated self-experience, one willed, the other suffered. Meanwhile Molly associates Stephen with Bloom's statue of Narcissus, the beautiful young boy who sees—and desires—but does not recognize himself. Of course, Stephen's narcissism is such that he is capable of recognizing himself in everyone. "Every life is many days, day after day. We walk through ourselves, meeting robbers, ghosts, giants, old men, young men, wives, widows, brothers-in-love. But always meeting ourselves" (175). Narcissism in this sense is a species metempsychosis, which is what Joycean mirror-play parodies, as when life and language join in their respective "retrospective arrangements" in "Oxen of the Sun":

> What is the age of the soul of man? As she hath the virtue of the chameleon to change her hue at every new approach, to be gay with the merry and mournful with the downcast, so too is her age changeable as her mood. No longer is Leopold, as he sits there, ruminating, chewing the cud of reminiscence, that staid agent of publicity and holder of a modest substance in the funds. He is young Leopold, as in a retrospective arrangement, a mirror within a mirror (hey, presto!), he beholdeth himself. That young figure of then is seen, precociously manly, walking on a nipping morning from the old house in Clambrassil street to the high school, his book satchel on him bandolierwise, and in it a goodly hunk of wheaten loaf, a mother's thought. Or it is the same figure, a year or so gone over, in his first hard hat (ah, that was a day!), already on the road, a full-fledged traveler for the family firm, equipped with an orderbook, a scented handkerchief (not for show only), his case of bright trinketware (alas, a thing now of the past!), and a quiverful of compliant smiles. (337)

A "retrospective arrangement" indeed, but "hey, presto" the mirror is breathed on (as per 337), and "the young knighterrant recedes, shrivels, to a tiny speck in the mist. Now he is himself paternal and these about him [Stephen, Mulligan, Lynch, others] might be his sons. Who can say? "'The wise father knows his own child'" (337). Suppose Bridie Kelly ("for a bare shilling")?—

> Bridie! Bridie! He will never forget the name, ever remember the night, first night, the bridenight. They are entwined in nethermost darkness, the willer and the willed, and in an instant (*fiat!*) light shall flood the world. Did heart leap to heart? Nay, fair reader. In a breath, 'twas done but—hold! Back! It must not be! In terror the poor girl flees away through the murk. She is the bride of darkness, a daughter of night. She dare not bear the sunnygolden babe of day. No Leopold! Name and memory solace thee not. That youthful illusion of thy strength was taken from thee and in vain. No son of thy loins is by thee. There is none now to be for Leopold, what Leopold was for Rudolph. (338)

III. The Mirror of Metaphor

Of course, repression of self-regard is never the whole story because whatever is repressed always returns—not *as itself*, to be sure, but *as something else*. This is what Paul Ricoeur means when he says in his book on Freud that "metaphor is nothing other than repression, and vice versa" (1970: 402). Metaphor gives us in the language of words what repression gives us in the economy of desire, namely a distortion or substitution whereby that which is denied *as itself* makes its appearance under disguise, to everyone's satisfaction. That which is separated in repression is always separated into a dynamic relationship—into a dialectic of departure and return that enables us to experience something forbidden, impossible, lost, out of the question, unthinkable, unlooked-for, but nevertheless devoutly wished.

Here is an example from the story "Clay," when Maria looks at herself in the mirror:

> She went into her little bedroom and, remembering that the next morning was a mass morning, changed the hand of the alarm from seven to six. Then she took off her working skirt and her house-boots and laid her best skirt out on the bed and her tiny dress-boots beside the foot of the bed. She changed her blouse too and, as she stood before the mirror, she thought of how she used to dress for mass on Sunday morning when she was a young girl; and she looked with quaint affection at the diminutive body, which she has so often adorned. In spite of its years she found it a nice tidy little body. (Joyce 1996: 101)

It is probably impossible for a reader not to look at Maria more clinically than she looks at herself because, after all, there is little to see, at least from the outside. She is an old spinster, the tip of whose nose nearly touches the tip of her chin, especially when she laughs. Moreover, I do not think Maria is in any way deceived about the fact that she is something of a crone, but her mirror doubles as a mirror of memory, allowing her to regard her small body as that of a young girl's. Think of her moment before the mirror as a moment of play that allows her to take pleasure in what she sees despite her years. Maria does not see herself as others see her, and that is the secret of her self-possession, even in her encounter with the clay. What is repressed in Maria's case is not the reality of her appearance—although she does not, you might notice, look at herself in the face; but perhaps empirically, she is just invisible to herself. What is repressed, or anyhow never was, is a life of desire that her playful moment before the mirror allows her to experience and, in a sense, to fulfill. Real life provides no such moments of meaningful appearance. I take this sense of fulfillment to be artful and romantic. Standing before the mirror, Maria looks at herself with "quaint affection" as someone not merely to be dressed but to be adorned; standing before the mirror, she adorns herself as a young and royal beauty like the one she impersonates in her song:

> I dreamt that I dwelt in marble halls
>   With vassals and serfs at my side
> And of all who assembled within those walls
>   That I was their hope and their pride.
> I had riches too great to count, could boast
>   Of a high ancestral name,
> But I also dreamt, which pleased me most,
>   That you loved me still the same. (106)

How different, at all events, from the poor Stephen-like boy in "Araby" ("gazing up into the darkness, I saw myself as a creature driven and deluded by vanity" [35]). But in either case, self-encounter is a phenomenological experience. Meanings trump (or, no, determine) sensations.

I pause here for a brief digression on self-deception, as elucidated by the philosopher Amélie Rorty, who argues as follows:

> Only a presumptively integrated person who interprets her system-of-relatively-independent-subsystems through the first *picture of the self,* only a person who treats the independence of her constituent subsystems as

failures of integration, is capable of self-deception. Not everyone has the special talents and capacities for self-deception. It is a disease only the strong minded can suffer. (1988: 25)

In other words, only an especially strong-minded person—someone philosophically committed to the principle (and imaginative possibility) of self-integration —is capable of self-deception. Following this thesis, it might be possible to argue that Maria is perhaps the most self-conscious and internally coherent character in all of Joyce's fiction, precisely because she is able to experience herself as a whole person free of self-contradiction: in other words, an anti-Stephen. Imagine Stephen as inferior in imagination to Maria! One could say that Stephen lacks the Nietzschean strength of self-creation that Michel Foucault champions in his later writings and that Maria accomplishes before her mirror.[8]

IV. Gerty in Bloom

With this paradox in mind, it makes sense to speak of Gerty McDowell in connection with Maria. Gerty's daydreams are never to be realized, but she is at home with her mirror image, as when adorning herself with a certain hat as suggested by the *Lady Pictorial*: "She did it up all by herself and what joy was hers when she tried it on then, smiling at the lovely reflection which the mirror gave back to her!" (Joyce 1986: 287). But in "Nausicaa" Gerty is perhaps most fully herself (most fully integrated) in the reflection of Bloom's gaze. In Bloom, Gerty can see herself, not as she is, but as she constructs herself, namely as a creature of seductive power, despite every empirical obstacle that nature and culture have conspired to throw in her way. And so she strikes a pose before Bloom as before a portrait painter (of sorts):

> She gazed out towards the distant sea. It was like the paintings that man used to do on the pavement with all the coloured chalks. . . . And while she gazed her heart went pitapat. Yes, it was her he was looking at and there was meaning in his look. His eyes burned into her as though they would search her through and through, read her very soul. Wonderful eyes they were superbly expressive, but could you trust them? People were so queer. She could see at once by his dark eyes and his pale intellectual face that he was a foreigner, the image of the photo she had of Martin Harvey, the matinee idol, . . . but she could not see whether he had an aquiline nose or a slightly *retroussé* from where he was sitting. He was in deep mourn-

ing, she could see that, and the story of a haunting sorrow was written on his face. . . . Here was that of which she had so often dreamed. (293)

And as for Bloom:

When you feel like that you often meet what you feel. Liked me or what? Dress they look at. . . . Saw something in me. Wonder what. Sooner have me as I am than some poet chap with bearsgrease, plastery hair lovelock over his dexter optic. To aid gentleman in literary. Ought to attend to my appearance at my age. Didn't let her see me in profile. (302)

It is enough to say that Bloom and Gerty mirror one another, not as they are, but as mutual self-creations in behalf of impossible desires. "See her as she is spoil all" (303), says Bloom. Reality allows little room for desire, but desire cannot bear too much reality anyway. Joyce's response seems to be: What's wrong with that? The category of *as is* is a category of repression, whereas the category of *as another* is the category of return. "Saw something in me," says Bloom. Just so: a merely empirical or literal reflection of himself as in the tide-pool invites instinctive self-erasure. In Gerty's regard, however, Bloom is able to see a version of himself that he can bear: Gerty's eyes substitute for his own, as do Bloom's for hers, and this enables a visibility between them: "When you feel that," he says, thinking of people tossed aside for someone else, "you often meet what you feel." Meanwhile Bloom's regard expresses and confirms Gerty's ideal self-image:

That strained look on her face! A gnawing sorrow is there all the time. Her very soul is in her eyes and she would give worlds to be in the privacy of her own familiar chamber where, giving way to tears, she could have a good cry and relieve her pentup feelings. Though not too much because she knew how to cry nicely before the mirror. You are lovely, Gerty, it said.[9] (288)

Or, to put it another way, "it was," Bloom says, "a kind of language between us" (305): not real speech, of course, only a manner of speaking formed by a casual, tacit, improvised agreement to (what?) regard one another mistakenly, under the cover of assumed or imagined identities. For Gerty, Bloom is the image of an image, that of a matinee idol; Bloom says: "Gerty they called her. Might be a false name however" (305), like his "Henry Flower." (The regulative question of "Nausicaa" is: "But who was Gerty?" [285]. She is, like everyone in *Ulysses*, caught between the hyperbole of desire and the understatement of how things are. But of course this supposes that we, readers, know how things are—surely a premature judgment.) At least Gerty is able to lead a Henry Flower form of life, and she belongs for a while to Bloom's Henry Flower life, where beautiful seaside girls entice.[10] At least Bloom and Gerty release one another's "pentup feelings." Odysseus was never happier than during his encounter with Nausicaa. What if there were less irony in Joyce's fiction than critical tradition has instructed us to believe?

One can cushion this question with a critical-formal gloss. As between Maria and her reflection in the mirror this language between Gerty and Bloom is metaphorical—a game that allows experience to occur in the absence of any warrant for it. The word "warrant" appears here by design (it is a legal term). The crucial relationship in metaphor is not (just) between differences but between authorized and unauthorized versions of whatever is the case. Recall the old rhetorician's distinction between authority and license in the matter of poetic language. Poetic language is language that goes on despite its empirical shortfall in matters of true or false—in contrast to a certain view of philosophical language (at least in its propositional form), which is authoritative for assertions that can be voted up or down. "The law is an ass" is not a legal proposition. Of course, neither are metaphorical statements outright lies; they are statements that can be seen to fit (or disclose) the world we inhabit without being logically true or false as a matter of fact. Metaphorical statements cannot stand by themselves or on their own authority; they cannot be taken as they stand but require a special construction to support them—a support language that need not be spelled out but can remain implicit like a context or background, without which we would never know what a nuance is. Recontextualization may be our only reliable source of intelligibility.

However, Joyce's metaphors are more complex and interesting than any theory could be (theories of metaphor suffer uniformly from the poverty of their examples; the rule of metaphor is absurdly satisfied when the law is simply an ass). We are taught in school that a metaphor is a linguistic phenomenon, and it is, but not in the literal sense of having just to do with words and how we combine them (substitution v. contiguity). After all, so far I have not been talking about Joyce's language but about his characters and how they regard themselves, or are regarded, in certain situations of complexity. Imagine metaphor as a form of life rather than as a form of logic. The truth about metaphor that we can learn from Joyce is that it is a way of making sense of things (and people) at ground level—as they go by, for everything in Joyce's fiction is in motion.

Metaphor is perhaps just a way of dealing with the temporality of existence. It is more phenomenological than logical, rhetorical, or poetical. Joyce's characters are metaphorical just in the sense that they experience themselves and others—and their world—now one way, now another, as situations change, with nothing ever settling fixedly into place. Joyce is perhaps more Ovid than Homer. The question that keeps turning up in his fiction is this: How do we take things when we are not in a position to take them as they are in themselves or from a stable point of view? Our position, like that of Joyce's characters, is always relative and contingent, subject to randomness relieved occasionally—or, if truth be told, repeatedly—by coincidence (or metaphor). Parallax defines Joyce's ontology. One could say that Joyce's view of things resembles that of a Nietzschean for whom human finitude is inescapable and transcendence inaccessible except to Yeatsians in their folly; but this does not mean that the human world is just chaotic and inscrutable, with nothing leading anywhere. Joyce's world is notoriously overdetermined, since everything in it is (Nietzsche-like) interpretable otherwise, depending on what pattern turns up, so that even when nothing is certain and nothing can be taken as it stands (since nothing stands still), Joyce's characters are always making sense of things, unlike the poor creatures in Kafka's fiction, surrounded and hounded as they are by unknowable laws.

V. The Mirror of Freedom

It is possible to complicate these speculations by turning to "Eveline." A moment ago I made (much too casual) use of the concept of the repressed and the metaphorical structure of its return. The story of Eveline shows this matter in a special way, as of someone caught in the infinite distance between two different mirrors. Recall that when Eveline looked at herself through her *mother's* eyes— when "the pitiful vision of her mother's life [laid] its spell on the very quick of her being—that life of commonplace sacrifices closing in final craziness"—she rose up "in a sudden impulse of terror. Escape! She must escape! Frank would save her. He would give her life, perhaps love, too" (1969: 40); anyhow, he would sweep her away to Buenos Aires. However, at the critical moment her father's perspective asserts itself. Her father, we can say, is someone who sees things as they are, or anyhow as they usually are said to be and how we have no reason to expect them to be otherwise: thus, he, her father, just knows that Eveline's young man Frank is another sailor (a mirror of sailors) who will do what sailors do: seduce an Irish virgin and abandon her in Liverpool. And so she freezes in a kind of Kierkegaardian moment of infinite possibilities, where all is lost:

A bell clanged upon her heart. She felt him seize her hand:

—Come!

All the seas of the world tumbled about her heart: he would drown her. She gripped with both hands at the iron railing.

—Come!

No! No! No! It was impossible. Her hands clutched the iron in frenzy. Amid the seas she sent a cry of anguish!

Eveline! Evvy!

He rushed beyond the barrier and called her to follow. He was shouted at to go on but still he called to her. She set her white face to him, passive, like a helpless animal. Her eyes gave him no sign of love or farewell or recognition. (41)

If you want to know what the world is like apart from the way we figure it, here you begin to get your answer: it would be as if the world were not there for us to experience it. We would look at it like Eveline at Frank with no sign of recognition in our eyes. Imagine Frank as, suddenly, an empty mirror—the mirror image of Eveline's eyes. A sign of recognition, however dubious, means taking something *as* something, not just as the resemblance of a brute object but as a passage through a looking glass. (Escape: what every Dubliner desires. Alas, "think you're escaping and run into yourself" [1986: 309].) So who, or what, is Frank? We could say that it depends on who has eyes to see, which is perhaps what experts mean when they say that repression follows the Law of the Father.

Freed of this law, we enter the "Circe" episode of *Ulysses*, in which everything is as it meets the eye and is not to be taken otherwise, in contrast to "Eumaeus," where every word produces a new discrepancy. You might say that in "Circe" whatever can be put into language *is* the case, whereas in "Eumaeus" everything is at odds with itself, except occasionally to sidelong glances ("he looked sideways in a friendly fashion at the sideface of Stephen, image of his mother" [541]). Imagine a distinction between true and false mirrors (but how would we know the difference?).

Here is a typical stage direction from "Circe":

(*From left upper entrance with two sliding steps Henry Flower comes forward to left front centre. He wears a dark mantle and drooping plumed sombrero. He carries a silver stringed inlaid dulcimer and a longstemmed bamboo Jacob's pipe, its clay bowl fashioned as a female head. He wears dark velvet hose and silverbuckled pumps. He has the romantic Saviour's face with flowering locks, thin beard, and moustache. His spindlelegs and sparrow feet are those of the tenor Mario, prince of Candi. He settles down his goffered ruffs and moistens his lips with a passage of his amorous tongue.*)

HENRY

(*In a low dulcet voice, touching the strings of his guitar.*)

There is a flower that bloometh. (421–22)

To the great Joycean question "what's in a name?," the "Circe" episode answers: "What's your pleasure?" What the name "Henry Flower" contains is everything, including what a Henry Flower would look like were all stops pulled, fulfilling and, in fact, surpassing our desire (and not just ours) to see what otherwise could never make its appearance because, if truth be told, whatever cannot make its appearance does not exist (the moral of Caliban's rage). If Maria from "Clay" were to appear in "Circe," she would do so as a young beauty adorned for a client. If meanwhile a mirror appeared, as it does when Bloom looks through a keyhole at Molly and Boylan in their ecstasy—

LYNCH

(*Points.*) The mirror up to nature. (*He laughs.*) Hu hu hu hu hu hu hu.

(*Stephen and Bloom gaze in the mirror. The face of William Shakespeare, beardless, appears there, rigid in facial paralysis, crowned by the reflection of the reindeer antlered hatrack in the hall.*) (463)

A single image gives us a surplus of identities: a Dublin paralytic, a portrait of the artist as a young man, and a poor cuckold; or, if you prefer, a portrait of three bards in one, duplicating the doctrine of the Trinity: Shakespeare, Stephen, Bloom—yes, three: see Bloom as Byron, as Molly once did when young Bloom "was trying to look like him" (612). (I cannot help thinking here of Stephen's Shakespearean self-reflection in the "Scylla and Charybdis" episode: "I, entelechy, form of forms, and I by memory because under everchanging forms" (156).

In "Eumaeus," however, nothing is anything, and the reason is given by Stephen: "Sounds are impostures, Stephen said after a pause of some little time. Like names, Cicero, Podmore, Napolean, Mr Goodbody, Jesus, Mr Doyle, Shakespeare. Shakespeares were as common as Murphy. What's in a name?" (509). In "Circe," names are magical mirrors that can conjure whom or whatever is called—Henry Flower, Rudy Bloom, a bar of soap, a hand writing on the wall, dancing hours, or Boylan's boots." In "Eumaeus," names are misnomers misapplied to the people who bear them. Murphy, for example, identifies Simon Dedalus as a sharpshooter in Hengler's Circus. "Curious coincidence," says Bloom (510).[11] Meanwhile, an "alias," thinks Molly, is "a mendacious person mentioned in sacred scripture" (562). In "Circe," everything "comes to pass"; in "Eumaeus," "egregious balderdash" sums it up (641). No one can be sure of anything, so like Bloom, we should be guided by the law of improbability, which "Circe" happily overturns, being a flawless execution of a Strindbergian dreamplay.

And Molly? She has reached the age (thirty-three, going on thirty-four) when mirrors can no longer be trusted (618). Fortunately, memory (like daydreams) is the better mirror:

> he was watching me whenever he got an opportunity at the band on the Alameda esplanade when I was with father and Captain Grove I looked up at the church first and then at the windows then down and our eyes met I felt something go through me like all needles my eyes were dancing I remember after when I looked at myself in the glass hardly recognized myself the change I had a splendid skin from the sun and the excitement like a rose I didn't get a wink of sleep. (622)

This is Molly in Gibraltar, at age fifteen—Milly's age as of June 15, 1904. Just so, as Molly is the mirror of her mother, Lunita Loredo (627), so is Milly of Molly: "Of course shes restless knowing shes pretty with her lips so red a pity they wont stay that way I was too" (631): and likewise self-willed—"I was just like that myself they daren't order me about the place" (632):

> her tongue is a bit too long for my taste your blouse is open too low she says to me the pan calling the kettle blackbottom and I had to tell her not to cock her legs up like that on show on the windowsill before all the people passing they all look at her like me when I was her age. (631)

And Milly?

> O, Milly Bloom, you are my darling.
> You are my lookingglass from night to morning.
> I'd rather have you without a farthing
> Than Katey Keogh with her ass and garden. (51)

Milly exists for us in the mirror of Bloom's mind, where she is, among other things, the mirror image of Bloom's cat (569) but also inevitably a younger version of Molly, unfaithful to him (so he worries) with a "young student" who sings, of all things, "Boylan's (I was on the pop of writing Blazes Boylan's) song about those seaside girls" (54). Recall the ominous line in "Telemachus" that suggests that Milly has fallen into Mulligan's world ("I got a card from Bannon. Says he found a sweet young thing down there. Photo girl he calls her" [18]). But at day's end it comes for Bloom down to teeth: "Very same teeth she has. What do they love? Another themselves?" (310–11). *Ulysses* celebrates the reign of Narcissus.

Let me conclude by citing the French philosopher Emmanuel Levinas, whose essay "Reality and Its Shadow" (1948) provides a nice gloss upon these proceedings:

> Being is not only itself, it escapes itself. Here is a person who is what he is; but he does not make us forget, does not absorb, cover over entirely the objects he holds and the way he holds them, his gestures, limbs, gaze, thought, skin, which escape from under the identity of his substance, which like a torn sack is unable to contain them. Thus a person bears on his face, along side of its being with which he coincides, its own caricature, its picturesqueness. . . . There is a duality in this person . . . a duality in its being. It is what it is and it is a stranger to itself, and there is a relationship between these two moments. . . .
>
> It is an ambiguous commerce with reality in which reality does not refer to itself but to its reflection, its shadow. . . .
>
> A being is that which is, that which reveals itself in its truth, and, at the same time, it resembles itself, is its own image. (1971: 6)

We are, in other words, not at all subjects as philosophy traditionally pictures us—minds without bodies. Levinas is closer to Joyce than to his philosophical forebears. My face is not the locus of my self-identity: it is my shadow, a surplus me, an alter ego that exposes me to the world and to others in it just in the sense that, Stephen-like, I have little or no control over my image and resemblance, which is always in the world before me. Or, as Levinas sometimes has it, I am always a little bit behind myself, never quite all myself at once but always immersed in a state of reflection: I am a mirror of myself, a poor resemblance, but mine own. This explains why there is something cadaverous about me, since what I inhabit is the intransparent distance between reality and its shadow.

Likewise in Joyce's fiction everyone is in a mirror in which "I" is never "I" but also "me," where the relationship between "I" and "me" is never a relationship of sameness or identity, because the "me" is always in the condition of the accusative, the one to whom things happen—the one who is not a philosophical subject (the "I" of cognition) but is always subject to others: the "me" is one who is seen rather than the observer occupying the privileged seat of surveillance as when, at last, in "Ithaca," Bloom returns home to his mirror:

> What composite asymmetrical image in the mirror then attracted his attention?
> The image of a solitary (ipsorelative) mutable (aliorelative) man.
> Why solitary (ipsorelative)?
>> *Brothers and sisters he had none,*
>> *Yet that man's father was his grandfather's son.*
> Why mutable (aliorelative)?
> From infancy to maturity he had resembled his maternal procreatrix.
> From maturity to senility he would increasingly resemble his paternal procreator. (1986: 581)

At which point, Bloom, being Bloom, averts his eyes.

Epilogue

On Incompletion (Stopping Briefly with Gertrude Stein)

The fragment involves . . . an essential incompletion.
—Philippe Lacoue-Labarthe and Jean-Luc Nancy *The Literary Absolute*

Maurice Blanchot's *The Infinite Conversation* begins, appropriately, with a dilatory conversation between two (interminably) old friends—dilatory because one of them had "nothing to say," while the other, dooming from the start the classical model, "had forgotten how to question" (1993a: xix). To make matters worse, or anyhow more idiopathic, the one friend "had lost the power to express himself in a continuous manner, as one would properly, either by conforming to the coherence of a logical discourse through the succession of this intemporal time that belongs to a mind at work, to one seeking identity and unity, or by yielding to the uninterrupted movement of writing" (xxi)—a movement frequently afflicted by an inability to stop, or even "to interrupt what is being written" (1982: 25).

The two friends belong to an anarchic time that neither begins nor ends—not the Epicurean *Chronos* but rather the Stoic *Aion*, which (in Gilles Deleuze's version), "endlessly subdivides the [present] event and pushes away past as well as future, without ever rendering them less urgent. The event is that no one ever dies, but has always just died or is always going to die, in the empty present of the Aion, that is, in eternity" (1990: 63).

Recall this famous passage from Gertrude Stein (recalling in 1926 her composition of *Melanctha* [1909]):[1]

> A composition of a prolonged present is a natural composition in the world as it has been these past thirty years it was more and more a prolonged present. I created then a prolonged present naturally I knew nothing of a continuous present but it came naturally to me to make one, it was simple

it was clear to me and nobody knew why it was done like that, I did not myself although naturally to me it was natural.

After that I did a book called *The Making of Americans* it is a long book about a thousand pages. (1971: 25)

Or, as Stein says in "The Gradual Making of *The Making of Americans*" (1934–35): "And I went on and on and then one day after I had written a thousand pages, this was in 1908 I just did not go on any more" (95). The book stops, but does not end—it is, after all, a book of descriptions, and "description is really unending" (96).[2] In "Poetry and Grammar," Stein says simply "that writing should go on" and that periods are rather like points of passage than marks of conclusion:

> Inevitably no matter how completely I had to have writing go on, physically one had to again and again stop sometime and if one hand had to again and again stop some time then periods had perhaps to exist. Beside I had always liked the look of periods and I liked what they did. Stopping sometime did not really keep one from going on, it was nothing that interfered, it was only something that happened, and as it happened as a perfectly natural happening, I did believe in periods and I used them. (130)

"I did believe in periods"—not for grammatical purposes, that is, not as a way of making sentences ("if you think in sentences you are not easily pleased" [1975: 49]) but rather as a point that can be deferred indefinitely into the semblance of a paragraph:

> When I wrote *The Making of Americans* I tried to break down this essential combination [of, for example, nouns and verbs] by making enormously long sentences that would be as long as the longest paragraph and so to see if there was really and truly this essential difference between paragraphs and sentences, if one went far enough with this thing with making the sentences long enough to be as long as any paragraph and so producing in them the balance of a paragraph not a balance of a sentence, because of the course the balance of a paragraph is not the same as the balance of a sentence. (1971: 234)

For example (forgive the endless citations, but the following is quintessential):

> In loving someone is jealous, really jealous and it would seem an impossible thing to the one not understanding that the other one could have

about such a thing a jealous feeling and they have it and they suffer and they weep and sorrow in it and the other one cannot believe it, they cannot believe the other one can really mean it and something the other one perhaps comes to realize it that the other one can really suffer in it and then later that one tries to reassure the other one the one that is then suffering about that thing and the other one the one that is receiving such reassuring says then, did you think I ever could believe this thing, no I have no fear of such a thing, and it is all puzzling, to have one kind of feeling, a jealous feeling, and not have a fear in them that the other one does not want them, it is a very mixing thing and over and over again when you are certain it is a whole one some one, one must begin again and again and the only thing that is a help to one is that there is really so little fundamental changing in any one and always every one is repeating big pieces of them and so sometimes perhaps some one will know something and I certainly would like very much to be that one and so now to begin. (1972: 305)

Here ("one must begin again and again") is a sentence that is, to speak strictly, not really a sentence but, as Lyotard would say, a series of *phrases*, where phrases are assemblages that "can obey regimens other than the logical and the cognitive" (1988: 65). In other words, they can be linked any or every which way and need never stop except perhaps "now to begin." Whence it follows that "grammar may be serially hampered" (1975: 38), as in "Arthur a Grammar," whose phrases are events even more singular and refractory than they are in *The Making of Americans*, as if a single word could count as a phrase:

> Irrigation somnolent undefined remittance planned cake from in justice dumbfounded eluded better messes in mistaken in undeniable rapid hourly a grass polish mistaken for the finish extra mischance fashioned opposite alone theirs in eradication does amount plainly to be divested in collusion indefatigable radiant piled committed to theirs tens in reference to just as well privately does permission even allow a rent before double leaves out pass it can very well pass in between fine which is colored silly are there argument announce establish rubber with it post around mingled possibly to be come whether well around alone it is called how or endowed mainly fished appoint the which fairly is it in a token come to come at a table top. (1975: 60–61)

One cannot help noticing the shortfall of nouns in this passage ("and therefore and I say it again more and more one does not use nouns" ["Poetry and Grammar," 1971 126]); and likewise the absence of commas ("I have refused them so often and left them out so much and did without them so continually that I have come finally to be indifferent to them" [1971: 131]).

Deleuze would say that Stein has disclosed the "mad element" in language—an element that, paradoxically, is "essential to language, as in the case of a 'flow' of speech, or a wild discourse which would incessantly slide over its referent without ever stopping" (1990: 2). So the passage above dissolves what philosophers would call its "aboutness" and allows words their material autonomy—imagine writing in behalf of *freedom* rather than according to the classical (or is it classroom?) norms of truth and beauty.

Or as William Gass says in "Gertrude Stein: Her Escape from Protective Language" (1971: 95):

> In her efforts to escape a purely protective language and make a vital thing of words, Gertrude Stein unsettled the whole of prose. Her abstractness enlarged the vocabulary of exciting words and made for some of the dullest, flattest, and longest literature in history. Her experiments in dissociation enlivened many dead terms and made her a master of juxtaposition.

Just so, Stein's writing reflects a poetics of insubordination, whether of words, clauses, or texts (v. contexts): a refusal of any sort of hierarchy (grammatical, philosophical, patriarchal)—Deleuze and Guattari would call her writing "rhizomatic" (as against "arborescent"), where "the rhizome is an acentered, non-hierarchical, non-signifying system" that moves laterally rather than linearly (1987: 21).

Except that the self-reflexive wordplay of the kind that Stein distinctively practices is never meaningless—

> Made at random.
> Is random a noun. It is not. It is a pleasure because with because which
> is an allowance with their and on account. ("Sentences," 1975: 188)

Rather, her writing possesses a formal intelligibility that arises, paradoxically, from the breaks and twists in the flow of her words, as in *Stanzas in Meditation* (1932):

> I have thought in thinking that is walking
> That the way to be often more than told in walking
> Is after all as much as told in walking
> That they as well will be just not to have

Theirs be theirs now. It is not only this a change
But theirs might be
I have lost the thread of my discourse. (1994: 155)

As a plain statement, the last line (comically) interrupts what precedes it by its very plainness, reminding us in the bargain that maintaining a thread, plot, train, or line of connection would be a relapse into the rule-governed predications from which Stein's writing, with its dissociations and juxtapositions, works to free itself.

This raises a final question as to how to think about contexts in Stein's writing. Probably one would not be far wrong to suggest that what counts as a context varies from work to work—for example, the "Portrait of Mabel Dodge at the Villa Curonia" (1911) resonates locally and historically in its details, even though Mabel Dodge herself nowhere appears, whereas "More Grammar for a Sentence" (1930), although evidently rich in allusions, reads more like an ars poetica ("nobody knows what I am trying to do but I do and I know when I succeed" [1993: 552]). It even contains something of a thesis, namely (once more) the superiority of paragraphs over sentences:

Why is a paragraph not natural. A paragraph is not it is not not natural a paragraph is not it is a paragraph and it is not as that that is as a paragraph to tell. Do tell why is a paragraph just as much as ever natural.

A paragraph is natural. They will mend by the time it is mended by the time. A paragraph is natural by the mended that it is by that time. This is not in used. A paragraph if they were occupied which they were there and care. It was foolish to care. Have to take care. Which they have to care.

A paragraph is natural that is it is that is is very well to know is very well known. Thank you for forgiving them to with him. (1993: 554)

But why, in contrast to a sentence, is a paragraph natural? Among other things:

A paragraph is naturally without a finish. (558)

It would be wonderful to conclude this "Aionic" line of thinking with this last citation, but unfortunately, Gertrude Stein probably would not allow it—after all, she concludes "More Grammar for a Sentence" (perhaps arbitrarily) with the following:

A paragraph finishes.
   This is it. (563)

Notes

Prologue

Epigraph. Schlegel (1991: 32).

1. Philippe Lacoue-Labarthe and Jean-Luc Nancy say that "what interests us in romanticism is that we still belong to the era it opened up" (1988: 15). See also Marshall Brown (1979); Azade Seyhan (1992); and Ernst Behler (1993). Two more recent studies also deserve close attention: Frederick Beiser (2003) and Manfred Frank (2003).

2. See Maurice Blanchot's essay "The Athenaeum" (1969: 352) on "the necessity of contradiction" as a distinctive feature of German romanticism: "Thereby characterized as the requirement or the experience of contradiction, romanticism does no more than confirm its vocation of disorder." And, again: "Discontinuous form: the sole form befitting romantic irony, since it alone can make coincide discourse and silence, the playful and the serious, the declarative, even oracular exigency and the indecision of a thought that is unstable and divided, finally, the mind's obligation to be systematic and its abhorrence of system" (358).

See also Seyhan (1992: 3): "Clearly positioning themselves against the representational conceit of philosophy and the noncontradiction rules of logic, the romantics demonstrate that the critical adventure of art and literature thrives on moments of discontinuity, rupture, and reversal."

3. Or, as Schlegel expresses it even more bluntly: "If one becomes infatuated with the absolute and simply cannot escape it, then the only way out is to contradict oneself continually and join opposing extremes together. The principle of contradiction is inevitably doomed" (Schlegel, *Blütenstaub* #3, 1991: 17).

4. See Judith Norman (2007); and Ayon Roy (2009). See also Kierkegaard's 1841 critique of romantics, "Irony after Fichte," (1989: esp. 285): "That both Germany and France at this time have far too many such ironists . . . surely no one will deny."

5. See Blanchot (1992: 215), where conversation is described as "plural speech": "A speech that is essentially non-dialectical; it says the absolutely other that can never be reduced to the same or take place in the whole."

6. See Novalis (Schulte-Sasse 1997: 102, and again, 107): "The I is only thinkable by means of a *Non-I*; for an I is only an I insofar as it is a Non-I. Otherwise it could be

whatever it wanted to be, it just wouldn't be an I." See also Elizabeth Mittman and Mary R. Strand (1997: 47–71).

7. See Haynes Horne (1997: 289–92) on Schlegel's "strategy of incompleteness."

8. See Jane K. Brown (2009: 119–31).

9. See Walter Benjamin (1996: 173):

Early Romanticism not only classified the novel as the highest form of reflection in poetry but, by setting it in a further, immediate relation to its basic conception of the idea of art, it found in it the extraordinary, transcendent confirmation of its aesthetic theory. According to this conception, art is the continuum of forms, and the novel, in the interpretation of the early Romantics, is the comprehensive manifestation of this continuum. It is this thanks to prose. The idea of poetry has found its individuality (that for which Schlegel was seeking) in the form of prose; the early Romantics know no deeper or better determination for it than "prose."

10. Loisa C. Nygaard (1988) has a good analysis of the formal complexity of Schlegel's novel. See also Ernst Behler's pages on *Lucinde* (1993: 289–98).

Chapter 1

Epigraph. Blanchot (1993a: 308, 1969: 453).

1. See Blanchot, "The Atheneum" (1993a: 351–59, 1969: 515–27).

2. Interestingly, a good deal of contemporary writing that calls itself "fragmentary" is, like Schlegel's fragments, aphoristic or (more often) structured like a notebook entry. See Dresher (esp. Giles Goodman's "Thought Experiments," 2006: 16):

all of the things that connect the body with thought before words . . .
a sentence that has never been spoken . . .
the sound a word makes when left alone . . . .

3. Schlegel, "Critical Fragments" Fr. 108 (1991: 13, 2013: 16).

4. See Lautman (1938: 34–35).

5. See Richard Sieburth's translation, "The Days of Socrates" (Hölderlin 1984: 219):

Time was God judged.

Kings.

Sages.

who judges now?

Is the entire people
judged? the holy congregation?

No! O No! who judges now
a race of vipers!   false and cowardly
the nobler word no longer
On the lips
O in the name of
Down, old demon!   I call you
Or   send
A hero
Or
Wisdom

6. "Dissolution" is an odd way of translating *Vergehen* (disappear, fade, pass away); it would be interesting to know why Hölderlin did not choose "*Das Werden im Auflösen*."

7. The poem dates from 1887 and was first published in book form by Gallimard in 1914. See Bruns (1997: 101–37). See Marcel Broodthaers, *Un coup de dés jamais n'abolira le hasard* (1969), which reproduces the visual layout of Mallarmé's poem but replaces the words with black lines.

8. Gass (1971: 93). See also Perloff (1981: 66–108, esp. 99–108), on *Tender Buttons* as a Dadaist poem; and Wasserstrom (1975: 90–106).

9. See Lyotard (1988: 65–66) on "phrasing":

100. The phrase that expresses the passage operator employs the conjunction *and* (*and so forth, and so on*). This term signals a simple addition, the apposition of one term with another, nothing more. Auerbach ([*Mimesis*] 1946: ch. 2 and 3) turns this into a characteristic of the "modern" style, paratax, as opposed to classical syntax. Conjoined by *and*, phrases or events follow one another, but their succession does not obey a categorical order (*because; if, then; in order to; although* . . .). Joined to the preceding one by *and*, a phrase arises out of nothingness to link up with it. Paratax thus denotes the abyss of Not-Being which opens between phrases, it stresses the surprise that something begins when what is said is said. *And* is the conjunction that allows the constitutive discontinuity (or oblivion) of time to threaten, while defying it through its equally constitutive continuity (or retention). This is also what is signaled by the *At least one phrase* (No. 99). Instead of *and*, and assuring the same paratactic function, there can be a comma, or nothing.

See also Hoagland (2006).

10. Stein, "Poetry and Grammar" (1971: 131). "Arthur: A Grammar" contains only a handful of commas over the course of its seventy pages, usually with reason—e.g., "There is no resemblance, it is not what they remind them to be an interval like it" (Stein 1931: 91).

11. Meanwhile, recall Williams (1970: 16)—referring to his *Kora in Hell: Improvisations* (1918)—on "the brokenness of his composition": "The instability of these improvisations would seem such that they must inevitably crumble under the attention and become particles of a wind that falters."

12. See Perloff (1981: 181): "I would posit that Pound's basic strategy in the *Cantos* is to create a flat surface, as in a Cubist or early Dada collage, upon which verbal elements, fragmented images, and truncated bits of narrative, drawn from the most disparate contexts, are brought into collision."

13. See Drucker (1994: esp. 172): "Zdanevich atomized language below the level of the morpheme, not respecting the integrity of the existing roots, prefixes and suffixes, nor feeling that a sufficient investigation [of the poetic materiality of language] could be carried out merely through their recombination into words whose suggestivity derived largely through association with existing vocabulary."

14. See also Glazier (2001); Bechleitner (2005); Morris and Swiss (2006); and Kac, "Holopoetry" (2007: 129–56).

Chapter 2

Epigraph. Blanchot (*1950: 28,* 1988: 25).

1. On Beckett's indebtedness to Blanchot, see Bruns (1997: 20–24, esp. 20: "Shameless pilfering"). The relationship between Beckett and Blanchot is something of a vexed issue among Beckett scholars. See, for example, Shane Weller (2007: 22–29), who argues that, despite superficial resemblances, the two writers are "radically divergent." Later he offers a somewhat more nuanced assessment, if only in passing. (2013: 164–65). For more on this issue, see note 6 below. I have no doubt that Blanchot provided Beckett with the concepts and examples that helped him to free his writing from the monumental influence of James Joyce. However, my intention here is philosophical as well as historical; it is to read Beckett and Blanchot together in order to show how much of their fiction is concerned with the experience of language as such—language in its materiality, irreducible to any function of mediation. The materiality of language is a subject usually reserved for contemporary poetics (Bruns 2005), but in France in the 1940s it was already a topic of considerable currency, as Blanchot observed in his 1945 essay on the Surrealists: "For a long time, language had laid claim to a kind of particular existence: it refused simple transparency, it was not just a gaze, an empty means of seeing; it existed, it was a concrete thing and even a colored thing. Surrealists understand, moreover, that language is not an inert thing; it has a life of its own, and a latent power that escapes us" (1949: 93, 1995: 88). See also Blanchot's 1945 review of Brice Parain's *Recherches sur la nature et les fonctions du langage* (1942) (2001: 85–90, 1943: 102–8): "One of the aims of literature is to suspend the logical properties of language. . . . [It] seems to withdraw from language the properties that give it a linguistic meaning [*signification langagière*]" (1943: 90, 2001: 108).

2. See, however, Linda Jones Jenkins, who thinks that reading Beckett alongside Blanchot reveals "a certain laughter, if not comedy, that underlies Blanchot's own work" (1997: 1).

3. In an essay, "Crise de vers" (1895), Mallarmé writes: "If a poem is to be pure, the poet's voice must be stilled and the initiative taken by the words themselves, which will be set in motion as they meet unequally in collision. And in an exchange they will flame out like some glittering swath of fire sweeping over precious stone, and thus replace the audible breathing in lyric poetry of old—replace the poet's own personal and passionate control of verse" (1956: 40–41).

4. See Blanchot's review of Bataille's *L'expérience intérieure* (1943), "L'expérience intérieure" (1943: 47–54, 2001: 37–42). For a slightly different view of Blanchot's conception of a limit-experience, having more to do with Foucault than with Bataille, see Willits (2003: esp. 12–15).

5. See Blanchot, "Littérature et la droit à mort" [Literature and the right to death] (1949: 312–30, 1995: 322–44); and Bruns, "Poetry after Hegel: A Politics of the Impossible" (1997: 34–55).

6. See Samuel Beckett's letter to Alex Kaun (9/7/1939):

Is there something paralysingly holy in the vicious nature of the word that is not found in the elements of the other arts? Is there any reason why that terrible materiality of the word surface [*jene fürchterlich willkürliche Materialität der Wortfläche*] should not be capable of being dissolved, like for example, the sound surface, torn by enormous pauses, of Beethoven's seventh Symphony, so that through whole pages we can perceive nothing but a path of sound suspended in giddy heights, linking unfathomable abysses of silence? (Beckett 1983: 172)

7. See Bruns (1997: 21) and Willits (2003: esp. 92–121 and 200–201n6). Judging from his letters, Beckett began reading Blanchot in the late 1940s—in a letter dated October 28, 1948, Beckett thanks Duthuit for sending him an essay that Blanchot had published that year; and later, in the early 1950s, Beckett embarked on a translation of Blanchot's *Lautrémont et Sade*, together (interestingly) with some unidentified passages from Blanchot's introduction to *Faux pas* (almost certainly one of them being the passage cited above [Blanchot 1943: 11, 2001: 3]). See Beckett (2011: 219–21 and 221n11). See also Willits (2005: 257–68) and Weller (2013: 164).

8. See Blanchot's essay on Beckett's *L'innommable* (2003: 210–17, esp. 213): "*The Unnamable* is precisely experience lived under the threat of the impersonal, the approach of a neutral speech that speaks itself alone, that goes through one that hears it, that is without intimacy, excludes any intimacy, one that cannot be silenced, for it is the incessant, the interminable." See Bruns, "The Storyteller and the Problem of Language in Samuel Beckett's Fiction" (1969: 265–81).

9. Interestingly, by contrast, Michiko Tsushima emphasizes musicality, or more specifically the experience of the rhythmic character of language in Beckett's fiction, where rhythm is inevitably obsessive in its claim upon our ears (2003: esp. 46–55).

10. See Gasché (2011: 319–56).

11. Were there world enough and time, one could insert here some pages on Beckett's *How It Is* (1961), which Blanchot had no doubt read, and where a "structureless present appears to manifest itself in the attenuation of syntax" (Bruns 1971: 318):

> of this old tale quaqua on all sides then in me bits and scraps try and hear a few
> scraps two or three each time per day and night string them together make phrases
> more phrases the last how it was after Pim how it is something wrong there end
> of part three and last. (Beckett, 1964: 106–7)

12. Deleuze (1990: 60–63) and Sellars (2007: 177–205).

13. See Emmanuel Levinas's 1966 essay on *L'attente, l'oubli* (1996: 140–49, esp. 148), where he describes Blanchot's language as "a language of pure transcendence without correlation—like the waiting that nothing awaited yet destroys—noesis without noema—pure extra-vagance, a language going from one singularity to another without their having anything in common." There is a lengthy discussion of the historical and philosophical (principally Heideggerian) context of *L'attente, l'oubli* by Leslie Hill (2012: 103–70); see also Gregg (1994: 132–72); Holland (2010: 263–81); and Tsushima (2003: 79–123).

14. See Marjorie Perloff on Beckett's "disjunctive and repetitious paragraphs" in "Ill Seen Ill Said" (1985: 135–54).

15. See Blanchot, "The Narrative Voice (the 'he [il],' the neutral)":

> The narrative "he" [or "it," *il*], whether absent or present . . . marks the intrusion
> of the other—understood as neutral—in its irreducible strangeness and wild per-
> versity. The other speaks. But when the other speaks, *no one speaks* because the
> other, which we refrain from honoring with a capital letter that would determine
> it by way of a majestic substantive, as though it had some substantial or even
> unique presence, is precisely never the other. (1969: 564–65, 1993: 385; my italics)

16. See Heidegger (1971b: 59). See also Brater (1994: 138–41) and Johns (2010: 82 83).

Chapter 3

Epigraph. Heidegger (1971a: 31–32). By "resistance" Prynne has in mind the capacity of a thing to preserve its "individual particularity" (1962: 27) against our efforts to subsume it into a concept. "Difficulty," he says, "is the subjective counterpart to resistance" (1962: 27), that is, it is my experience of the way the singularity of the thing (or the person or, for all of that, the words of language) always exceeds my effort to reduce it to some cognitive or instrumental function.

1. See, for example, Wheale (2009: 163–85, esp. 180–81): "What kind of coherence and augmented meanings can we expect to find in such complex texts? There is so much to think about as you move from word to word and line to line in this poetry, working hard to construct larger, super-segmented meanings, and the poem always escaping." See also Jennifer Cooke (2007).

2. See Blanchot (1993a: 308) and Middleton (2004: 768–86).

3. See Marjorie Perloff on "citational poetics," esp. the chapter on Kenneth Goldsmith (2010: 146–65).

4. Parsegian (2006). The "forces" are named after the Dutch physicist Johannes Diderik van der Waals (1837–1923). For a discussion of scientific language in Prynne's work, see Middleton (2009: 947–58, esp. 953): "The scientific strip worn by the poem is much more disruptive of its workings than other types of citation," owing chiefly to "the rapid half-life of scientific documents and the knowledge they present. . . . This means that almost any allusion to scientific knowledge is likely to be out of date within a few years. The strip in the poem will look much more faded than the rest of the language around it."

5. See Maurice Blanchot on "The Narrative Voice" (1993a: 384): "The speech of the narrative always lets us feel that what is being recounted is not being recounted by anyone: it speaks in the neutral." On the place of the subject in Prynne's poetry, see Pietrzak (2012).

6. A brief account of the history and meaning of the term "dielectric" is given by Durga Misra (2011: 31). See also Huang (2003).

7. See Prynne's recent interview (2016: 196):

Kazoo was an unprecedented and unexpected kind of composition. I was very conscious that it was well out of line from anything I've tried to do before. It was full of an extremely complex system of self-contradictions which ought to produce serious disorder in the thought process, and I simply said to myself more or less consciously, I'm going to let it do that. I contradicted some of my deeply held beliefs and opinions.

8. "Bill Bailey, Won't You Please Come Home" was composed in 1902 by Hughie Cannon (1817–1912).

9. See Perloff, "The Invention of Collage" (1986: esp. 42–49).

10. Berg's lecture is available online at www.solmonsmusic.net/WozzeckLecture.html.

11. See Blanchot, "Interruption: As on a Riemann Surface" (1993a: 75–80).

12. Citation is from Borowski, "The Man with the Package" (1976).

13. Benjamin, "Program for Literary Criticism" (1999: 290): "A criticism entirely of quotations should be developed."

14. See Jarvis (2003) on Prynne's "The Monogram" (1997).

15. Citation is from Bradley (2002): "The Land, the Sky and the Scottish Stone Circle."

Chapter 4

Epigraph. Stein (1994: 36).

1. Re: "dissentience": the third stanza of "Harmolodics" reads as follows:

If our 1st contestant now would like to advance:
    Let's play, tell you what
  The sidemen honk over the bar-rail, 5
      whirring roses jig
through digital scanners, Rout & finish,
      all's well-good
dissentience which polishes their lineaments with
    master gloss on the major theme pillow
      As is, sold unseen,
surmounts the earlier score-card:
    Blockbusters!   Thank you: (*Flung Clear*, 1994: 125; my italics)

2. Not that "Harmolodics" is incoherent in the sense that it lacks *aboutness*, since allusions to jazz echo (in "rhythmic / gasps and bolts" [1994:128]) throughout the poem—

  Now play Cherokee.
But only, tell you what—
Shiny bricks add up to your private
    O the sweet relief: you'll feel its binding
sweat like chubby fingers,
      know how breathing Sheer Class
  parades through Harlem with its Selmer,
toots on a plastic horn: they'll rescue you from
fitted music. (126)

"Selmer": the name of a company that manufactures (real, not plastic) saxophones.

3. See Wilkinson (1994: 163–65). Wilkinson cites the opening lines of Bernstein's "The Manufacture of Negative Experience" (2001: 28):

My bread has some nerve. No
sooner does it come out of the oven
than I have to slap it for being
so fresh. My head has some
curve. No sooner does it run for
the patio than the lights begin
to jam, the commotion dies down

in the corridor outside the
farm administration building.

Interestingly, Wilkinson does not mention the work of his fellow Cambridge Poet, J. H.
Prynne. On Prynne's legendary difficulty, see Peter Middleton (1997: 344–53). See also
Templeton (2009: 133–44).

4. In contrast to the lyric "blues" of a John Wieners poem, Bernstein's persona is
that of a stand-up comic with a routine of wordplay.

5. Perhaps more representative of the formal character of the poems in this volume
is "BEL NUIT, NUIT D'AMOUR":

Tamara Tamounova   l o n g d i s t a n c e
Verona Arnoldo's press fortune salted the Astor smelling of Joel
Oppen   heimer and Silly Sorrentino swam Cooper Union
after Fiorama to melt Her
shey when Everett Lornemizama Leroi Jones tossed Yugen 5
flights off a
fire escape vista; was it this iriam "Monty" Arkansas sought
from her
pissoir on Medway; when Harrisburg Mornegon's welter
championed that
Murderer could not outlive his victims down the line the
Canterbury
gllstones wet more bidets than bistros supposing that Dure
d'Mecq slos
had combat zone Histories. (Wieners 1975: 42)

6. One can in fact listen to Wieners reading his poetry at Pennsound: http://writing
.upenn.edu/pennsound/x/Wieners.php.

7. See Sood (2010).

8. See Wilkinson's "Mouthing Off" (2007: 171): "Poems are not written necessarily
for a practice of close reading which can mop up all semantic spillage as it goes, although
I do think close reading is the essential skill for enjoying poems of the modern western
literary tradition. It's just that we need to be realistic about the conditions for close reading. We are always distracted by the light pollution of our preconceptions and social assemblies, and by our partiality and laziness."

9. See Solt's anthology of visual or concrete poetry (1968).

10. See Joseph Frank's celebrated essay, "Spatial Form in Modern Literature" (1945:
643–53).

11. A "maquette" in the first stanza is a French term for a scale model; "*en cocotte*" in

the third stanza is a baking dish, but the term is also applied to a prostitute; a "gimbal" (fifth stanza) is a pivot that allows the rotation of an object around a single axis; "callipers" in the final stanza is the name of a device used to measure the distance between opposite sides of an object, and "kevlar" in the next to the last line is a synthetic fiber said to be five times stronger than steel.

12. A "smalt" is a coloring agent made of silica, potassium carbonate, and cobalt oxide used to color vitreous materials.

Chapter 5

Epigraph. Raworth (2003: 252).

1. The museum guide is almost certainly a philosopher of sorts, perhaps in the manner of Simon Critchley, whose treatise *On Humour* is, in the end, an argument in behalf of the wry witticism against the Rabelaisian guffaw, or "the priority of smiling over laughter" (2007: 96).

2. William Carew Hazlitt's classic (1890) contains almost no examples in verse.

3. Doggerel is the preference of many poets who make up *The Oxford Book of Comic Verse* (Gross 1994). A poem by John Keats begins as follows:

There was a naughty boy
  And a naughty boy was he,
  For nothing would he do
  But scribble poetry. (114)

4. See also Stevens's "The Owl in the Sarcophagus" (1964: 431–36).

5. Cage (1961: 160).

6. Bernstein (1994: 15).

7. Pope (1963: 833).

8. Recall the philosopher Simon Critchley's preference for the smile over laughter (2007: 96).

Chapter 6

Epigraph. Bernstein (2000: 26); first published in *Parsing* (Asylum Press, 1976). See Bernstein, "I Love Speech! (or anyway, it's complicated): *Parsing* at 39" (2015). The first part of the book, "Sentences," is composed almost entirely from sentences taken from two sources and both are oral histories: "*Working* by Studs Terkel and *Yessir, I've Been Here a Long Time: Faces and Words of Americans* by George Mitchell. I lifted and arranged sentences from these vernacular speech transcriptions and placed them amidst sentences I generated myself. All the sentences in this first part are vernacular and start with an 'I' or a 'You' or an 'It.'"

1. In the early 1980s Hugh Kenner and Charles O. Hartman, with the help of Joseph O'Rourke (and, according to the title page, under the inspiration of Claude Shannon and

Jackson Mac Low) developed a computer program, called Travesty, which produced *Sentences*. Part 1 begins as follows:

SCHOOL
>Sentences for Analysis and Parsing Thayer Street
>Grammar School begins. James, bring me the
>vessel had been using that. Our little lame.
>He hurricane. The love of money is to prepare
>forsaken. Iron has brought it tremble. The young
>must do it is
>Sentences begins.
>money must
>Sentences
>Parsing
>Sentences
>Sentences
>Sentences for love forsaken. (1984: 7)

See Bernstein (2000: 7): "The time is not far off, or maybe it has already come to pass, when computers will be able to write better poems than we can. So we must now add to logopoeia, phanopoeia, and melopoeia, *algorhythmia*."

2. See Bernstein's reply to Jameson (1992: 90–105, esp. 91): "Juxtaposition of logically unconnected sentences or sentence fragments can be used to theatricalize the limitations of conventional narrative development, to suggest the impossibility of communication, to represent speech, or as part of a prosodic mosaic constituting a newly emerging . . . meaning formation" (my emphasis).

3. See Bernstein (2011: 174):

> For me the ordinary breaks down practically and philosophically into three separate, interrelated, but not entirey commensurate elements. One is the representation and objectification of everyday life. . . . Another is ordinary language philosophy (not only Ludwig Wittgenstein but also Michel de Certeau and Stanley Cavell). But there is a third issue, which is crucial in terms of poetry: *the transcription of spoken, everyday language,* which can be considered as a problem of poetic diction, or of the vernacular, or indeed of dialect. (my emphasis)

See also Bernstein (1992: 177) on "charting the verbal environment of the moment"; and Bernstein and Antin (2002: 50–51), on the *vernacular* as "fundamental to radical modernist writing." For a slightly different view, see Eng (2012: 35–54, esp. 39): "It is quite clear in Bernstein's writings that he does not share Wittgenstein's privileging of the everyday. On the contrary, he routinely calls out the quotidian forms of popular media . . . for the role they play in perpetuating what is in fact a metaphysics of the everyday." A "meta-physics of the everyday" is perhaps a bit of an overload, but Eng is certainly correct that Bernstein's interest is in the *public* vernacular, as Bernstein says (2011: 248): "A lot of the poem is pulled from the air, from signs in my mind and on the street, from what I am reading in the newspaper or hearing on the radio."

4. In the foreword to *The Claim of Reason* (1979: xix), Cavell says that writing part 4 of his book "was something I more and more came to regard, or to accept, even to depend upon, as the keeping of a limited philosophical journal. Writing it was like the keeping of a journal in two main respects: first, the autonomy of each span of writing is a more important goal than smooth, or any, transitions between spans (where one span may join a number of actual days, or occupy less than one full day). This ordering of goals tends to push prose to the aphoristic."

5. On the "Pataquerical Imagination," see Bernstein (2016: 293–345). "Pataquerics" takes off from Alfred Jarry (1873–1907), who coined the term "pataphysics," meaning "weird," "manic," "jumbled" (see Jarry 2001).

6. See the fascinating debate regarding Bernstein's unruly writing by Mack and Man-nejc (1991: 441–64).

7. Curiously, many of Bernstein's readers prefer the term "ironist" to that of comic poet. See, for example, Stephens (2012: 140–68).

8. See also Bernstein's "Of Time and the Line" (1991: 42):

George Burns likes to insist that he always
takes the straight lines; the cigar in his mouth
is a way of leaving space between the
lines for a laugh. He weaves lines together
by means of a picaresque narrative;
not so Henny Youngman, whose lines are strictly paratactic. My father pushed a
line of ladies' dresses—not down the street
in a pushcart but upstairs in a fact'ry
office.

9. Bernstein (1994: 132).

10. See "How Empty Is My Bread Pudding" (2013: 83–84): "I embrace a poetics of bewilderment. I don't know where I am going and never have, just try to grapple as best I can with where I am."

11. In a note Bernstein says: "'The Ballad of the Girly Man' was written on Labor Day weekend, 2004, in response to California governor Arnold Schwarzenegger's August 31 convention speech to the Republican National Convention, in which he taunted oppo-nents of the Republican Party agenda as "girly men" (2006: 185). See Peterson (2012: 18):

"Why does this poetry ['The Ballad of the Girly Man'] feel so different from Bernstein's earlier writing, yet so timely? What is it about the old form of multi-voiced Brechtian critique that seems no longer tenable after 9/11 for this poet?" Peterson's answer: "While the earlier Bernstein would have been terrified of the pathos in such gestures, here he appears to be quite serious, and the pathos against power is very much to the point" (26).

12. To explore the "worst"—to investigate the *experience* of it—Cavell took up the reading of Shakespearean tragedy, with an emphasis on the *reading* of Shakespeare's *King Lear*, which provides us with a critical distance that we lack when absorbed into its performance in a theater. See Cavell, "The Avoidance of Love: A Reading of *King Lear*" (1969: 213–14).

Chapter 7

Epigraphs. Levinas (1960: 73); Joyce (1958: 53.10–12).

1. See the chapter on "Cenography" in Craig Dworkin's *No Medium* (2013: 35–52) in which Dworkin discusses Nick Thurston's *The Remove of Literature* (2006), which is an "edition" of Ann Smock's English translation of Maurice Blanchot's *The Space of Literature* (1982), from which every word of Blanchot's text has been removed.

2. Mallarmé (1965a, I: 245–46, 1982: 88).

3. A number of classical studies of the *Wake* would dispute this, arguing that, for all of its virtuosities of language, the *Wake* remains essentially a work of narrative fiction. See, to begin with, Campbell and Robinson (1944); Tindall (1959); Gordon (1986); and, most recently, Epstein (2009). For counterarguments on this point, see Benstock (1966) and Hayman (1990: 41n4): "For all the efforts of critics to establish a plot for the *Wake*, it makes little sense to force this prose into a narrative mold."

4. See Kenner (1956: 301): "Literally nothing is left but words: slogans, speeches, maxims, captions, quotations, jingles, familiar phrases, borrowed rhythms, puns, puzzles, parodies"—all of them refashioned according to the model of Jabberwocky established by Charles Dodgson (a.k.a. Lewis Carroll), the prime forebear of words in the *Wake* and of HCE as well (Kenner 1956: 276–301). See also Attridge (1988: 193–210) on portmanteaus and puns in the *Wake* and Derrida (1984: 149):

[Joyce] repeats and mobilizes and babelizes the (asymptotic) totality of the equivocal, he makes this his theme and his operation, he tries to make outcrop, with the greatest possible synchrony, at great speed, the greatest power of the meanings buried in each syllabic fragment, subjecting each atom of writing to frisson in order to overload the unconscious with the whole memory of man: mythologies, religion, philosophies, sciences, psychoanalysis, literatures.

See also Schotter (2010: 89–101).

5. See, for example, Culler (1975) and Norris (1976: 120–21):

The formal [i.e., surface] elements of the work, plot, character, point of view, and language, are not anchored to a single point of reference, that is, they do not refer back to a center. This condition produces that curious flux and restlessness of the work. . . . The substitutability of the parts for one another, the variability and uncertainty of the work's structural and thematic elements, represent a decentered universe, one that lacks a center that defines, gives meaning, designates, and holds the structure together—by holding it to immobility.

6. See also Heath (1984: 50):

Ulysses, definitive end of the realist novel, . . . is the negation of the daylight world of the natural attitude; in its urge for totality, in its perpetual process of fragmentation and hesitation of the multiplicity of fictions it assembles, *Ulysses* begins to unlimit that world, replacing it in the intertext of the fictions of its construction. *Finnegans Wake* opens onto a further level, fixing a totality not through an encyclopaedism . . . but through an attention to the production of meaning.

7. See also Aubert (1984: 70):

"riverrun" seems to evoke the humming of a motor which is momentarily stuck or is building up tension; in order to free our reading, to transform this humming into an articulated sound, we must help the motor to get under way, and give it a throw; we will then be better able to see whether in fact something was locking, or whether there was only an excess of friction or a simple jamming of the cogs or components. We will then have to work out whether and how these images and others work coherently together, and what kind of mechanism this is.

By contrast, Derrida's contribution "Two Words for Joyce" figures both *Ulysses* and the *Wake* on the model of "a hypermnesiac machine" that "can, in a single instant or single vocable, gather up . . . cultures, languages, mythologies, religions, philosophies, sciences, history of mind and of literatures." Basically, it contains everything that anyone might think of saying. Imagine a "1000th generation computer . . . beside which the current technology of our computers and our micro-computerfied archives and our translation machines remains a *bricolage* of prehistoric child's toys" (1984: 147).

8. A time-honored and still viable way of "rationalizing" or "normalizing" the *Wake* is by way of genetic criticism—working back to beginnings and recovering stages or variable processes of the text's composition. See Crispi and Slote (2007).

9. Cage describes *Muoyce* as follows (1983: 173):

Muoyce (Music-Joyce) is with respect to *Finnegans Wake* what *Mureau* (Music-Thoreau) was with respect to the *Journal of* Henry David Thoreau, though *Muoyce*, like *Empty Words*, and unlike *Mureau* does not include sentences, just phrases, words, syllables, and letters. Following the ten thunderclaps, the rumblings, the portmanteau words, etc., of *Finnegans Wake*, punctuation is entirely omitted and space between words is frequently with the aid of chance operations eliminated.

10. See also Derrida (1984: 150); Hartman (1981); and Mahon (2007).

11. On Joyce and Bakhtin, see Kershner (1990) and Brooker (1997).

12. Here is an English translation by Suzanne Jill Levine and Jon Tolman (H. de Campos 2007: 122):

and here I begin I spin here the beguine I respin and begin
to release and realize life begins not arrives at the end of a trip
which is why I begin to respin to write-in thousand pages write thousandone pages
to end write begin write beginend with writing and so I begin to respin.

See Perloff (2004: 175–93) on Haroldo de Campos's *Galaxias*.

Chapter 8

Epigraph. Merleau-Ponty (1964: 168).

1. See Merleau-Ponty, "Intertwining—The Chiasm" (1968: 130–55, esp. 139).

2. See Merleau-Ponty, "'Association' and the 'Projection of Memories'" and "Other Selves in the Human World" (1962: 13–26, 346–65).

3. See, for example, L. Thurston (2010); Borg (2010); Azérad (2008); Brivic (2008); Boheemen (1999); Miller (1993); Leonard (1991). On Joyce and Lacan, particularly, see Žižek (1997).

4. One should also perhaps recall here Novalis, cited above in the preface and acknowledgments: "The I must be divided into order to be I" (Schulte-Sasse 1997: 102 and again 107): "The I is only thinkable by means of a *Non-I*; for an I is only an I insofar as it is a Non-I. Otherwise it could be whatever it wanted to be, it just wouldn't be an I."

5. On "Looking at Yourself in the Mirror," see Savardi and Bianchi (2005).

6. Cf. "Telemachus" (Joyce 1986: 34):

Reading two pages apiece of seven books every night, eh? I was young. You bowed to yourself in the mirror, stepping forward to applause earnestly, striking face. Hurray for the God-damned idiot! Hray! No-one saw: tell no-one. Books you were going to write with letters for titles. Have you read his F? O yes, but I prefer Q. Yes, but W is wonderful. O yes, W. Remember your epiphanies on green oval leaves, deeply deep, copies to be sent if you died to all the great libraries of the world, including Alexandria?

7. Not surely like the one reflected momentarily in Mulligan's eyes, a figure he has been changed into, complete with borrowed clothes: "Buck Mulligan turned suddenly for an instant towards Stephen but did not speak. In the bright silent instant Stephen saw his own image in cheap dusty mourning between their gay attires" (1986: 16).

8. See Foucault (1994: 262): "We have to create ourselves as a work of art."

9. Gerty would be someone to think about when confronting the fact that, by comparison with Joyce's other writings, there are not many mirrors in *Finnegans Wake*, which is, after all, a kind of sound poem. But Issy or her namesake, Nuvoletta (or Lucia Joyce), takes up Gerty's mirror play in the Mookse and Gripes episode of the *Wake*, but without Gerty's success:

> Nuvoletta listened as she reflected herself, through the heavenly one with his constellatria and his emanations stood between, and she tries all she tried to make the Mookse look up at her (but *he* was fore too adiaptotously farseeing) and to make the Gripes hear how coy she could be (though he was much to schystimatically auricular about *his ens* to heed her) but it was all mild's vapour moist. . . . She tried all her winsome wonsome ways her four winds had taught her. She tossed her sfumastelliacinous hair like *la princesse de la Petite Bretagne* and she rounded her mignons arms like Mrs Cornwallis-West and she smiled over herself like the beauty of the image of the image of the pose of the daughter of the queen of the Emperour of Irelande and she signed after herself as were she born to bride with Tristis Trisior Tristissimus. But, sweet madonine, she might fair as well have carried her daisy's worth to Florida. (1958: 157–58)

The Mookse and Gripes remain "pinefully obliviscent" to Nuvoletta's seductions. Shortly thereafter, interestingly, "a woman of no appearance" carries off the two of them (158). In despair, Nuvoletta throws herself into the river to the tune of Gerty's magazine idiom:

> And into the river that had been a stream (for thousands of years had gone eon her and come on her and she was stout and struck on dancing and her muddied name was Missisiliffi) there fell a tear, a singulet tear, the loveliest of all tears (I mean for those crylove fables fans who are 'keen' on the pretty-pretty commonface sort of thing you meet by hope harrods) for it was a leaptear. (159)

10. Compare "Sirens," where Bloom admires Miss Douce's image in a mirror:

> Bronze, listening by beerpull, gazed far away. Soulfully. Doesn't know I'm. Molly great dab at seeing anyone looking.
> Bronze gazed far sideways. Mirror there. Is that best side of her face? They always know. Knock at the door. Last tip to titivate. (Joyce 1986: 284)

11. Misnomers, or namesakes, seem to play like mirrors throughout much of *Ulysses*, as in "Wandering Rocks," as when Cashel Boyle O'Connor Tisdall Farrell strides past "Mr Bloom's dental windows" (Joyce 1986: 205).

Epilogue

Epigraph. Lacoue-Labarthe and Nancy (1988: 42).

1. On Gertrude Stein the following studies have helped guide my hand: Bridgman (1970); DeKoven (1983); Quartermain (1992: 21–43); Welch (1996); Dydo (2003); and Perloff (1996: 83–114).

2. One cannot help recalling an interesting passage on Matisse and Cézanne in *The Autobiography of Alice B. Toklas*: "[Matisse] used his distorted drawing as a dissonance is used in music or as vinegar or lemons are used in cooking. . . . However, this was his idea. Cézanne had come to his unfinishedness and distortion of necessity, Matisse did it by intention" (Stein 1961: 41).

Works Cited

Adorno, Theodor W. 1990. "Punctuation Marks." Translated by Shierry Weber Nicholsen. *Antioch Review* 48.3: 300–305.

———. 1992. *Notes to Literature.* Vol. 2. Translated by Shierry Weber Nicholsen. New York: Columbia University Press.

———. 1997. *Aesthetic Theory.* Translated by Robert Hullot-Kentor. Minneapolis: University of Minnesota Press.

Allegrezza, William, ed. 2012. *The Salt Companion to Charles Bernstein.* Norfolk, UK: Salt Publishing.

Althusser, Louis. 1970. *Reading Capital.* Translated by Ben Brewster. London: New Left Books.

Aristotle. 1984. *The Complete Works of Aristotle.* Vol. 1. Edited by Jonathan Barnes. Princeton, NJ: Princeton University Press.

Ashbery, John. 1957. "The Impossible." *Poetry* 90.4: 250–54.

———. 2007. *Notes from the Air: Selected Later Poems.* New York: Harper Collins.

Attridge, Derek. 1988. *Peculiar Language: Literature as Difference from the Renaissance to James Joyce.* Ithaca, NY: Cornell University Press.

Attridge, Derek, and Daniel Ferrer, eds. 1984. *Post-structuralist Joyce: Essays from the French.* Cambridge: Cambridge University Press.

Aubert, Jacques. 1984. "riverrun." In Attridge and Ferrer, *Post-structualist Joyce,* 69–77.

Auerbach, Erich. 2003. *Mimesis: The Representation of Reality in Western Literature.* Translated by Willard R. Trask. Princeton, NJ: Princeton University Press.

Azérad, Hugo. 2008. "Parisian Literary Fields: James Joyce and Pierre Reverdy's Theory of the Image." *Modern Language Review* 103: 666–81.

Badiou, Alain. 2007. *Dissymetries: On Beckett.* Translated by Nina Power and Alberto Toscano. Manchester, UK: Clinamen Press.

Bakhtin, Mikhail. 1981. *The Dialogic Imagination: Four Essays.* Translated by Caryl Emerson and Michael Holquist. Austin: University of Texas Press.

———.1984. *Problems of Dostoevsky's Poetics.* Translated by Caryl Emerson and Michael Holquist. Minneapolis: University of Minnesota Press.

Bataille, Georges. 1988. *Inner Experience.* Translated by Leslie Anne Boldt. Albany: SUNY Press.

———. 1991. *The Impossible*. Translated by Robert Hurley. San Francisco: City Lights Books.

———. 1992. *On Nietzsche*. Translated by Bruce Boone. New York: Paragon House.

beaulieu, derek. 2010. "Untitled (for Natalee and Jeremy)." In *Silence*, n.p. Achill Island, Ireland: Redfoxx Press.

———. 2013. "Afterword: Interview with derek beaulieu. In *Please, No More Poetry: The Poetry of derek beaulieu*, edited by Kit Dobson, 226. Waterloo, ON: Wilfrid Laurier University Press.

Bechleitner, Norbert. 2005. "The Virtual Muse: Forms and Theory of Digital Poetry." *Theory and Poetry: New Approaches to the Lyric*, edited by Eva Müller and Margarete Rubik, 303–44. Amsterdam: Rodopi Press.

Beckett, Samuel. 1949. "Three Dialogues." *transition* 5: 95–100.

———. 1964. *How It Is*. New York: Grove Press.

———. 1965. *Three Novels by Samuel Beckett: Malloy, Malone Dies, The Unnamable*. New York: Grove Press.

———. 1970. *Murphy*. New York: Grove Press.

———. 1983. Worstward Ho. London: Calder.

———. 1984. *Disjecta: Miscellaneous Writings and a Dramatic Fragment*. Translated by Ruby Cohn. New York: Grove Press.

———. 1992. *Nowhow On: Company, Ill Seen Ill Said, Worstward Ho*. London: Calder.

———. 1995. *The Complete Short Prose, 1929–1989*. Edited by S. E. Gontarski. New York: Grove Press.

———. 1996. *Nowhow On: Company, Ill Seen Ill Said, Worstward Ho. Three Novels by Samuel Beckett*. New York: Grove Press.

———. 2011. *The Letters of Samuel Beckett: 1941–1956*. Edited by George Craig, Martha Dow Fehsenfeld, Dan Gunn, and Lois More Overbeck. Cambridge: Cambridge University Press.

Behler, Diana. 1978. *The Theory of the Novel in Early German Romanticism*. Berne, Switzerland: Peter Lang.

Behler, Ernst. 1993. *German Romantic Literary Theory*. Cambridge: Cambridge University Press.

Beiser, Frederick. 2003. *The Romantic Imperative: On the Concept of Early German Romanticism*. Cambridge, MA: Harvard University Press.

Benjamin, Walter. 1996. *Selected Writings*. Vol 1, *1913-1926*. Edited by Marcus Bullock and Michael W. Jennings. Cambridge, MA: Harvard University Press.

———. 1999. *Selected Writings*. Vol. 2, *1927–1934*. Edited by Michael W. Jennings, Howard Eiland, and Gary Smith. Cambridge, MA: Harvard University Press.

Benstock, Bernard. 1966. *Joyce Again's Wake: An Analysis of "Finnegans Wake."* Seattle: University of Washington Press.

Berg, Alban. 1929. "Lecture on *Wozzeck*." www.solmonsmusic.net/WozzeckLecture.htm.

Bernstein, Charles. 1976. *Parsing*. New York: Asylum Press.

———. 1986. *Content's Dream: Essays, 1975–1984*. Los Angeles: Sun and Moon Press.

———. 1991. *Rough Trades*. Los Angeles: Sun and Moon Press.

———. 1992. *A Poetics*. Cambridge: Cambridge University Press.

———. 1994. *Dark City*. Los Angeles: Sun and Moon Press.

———. 1999. *My Way: Speeches and Poems*. Chicago: University of Chicago Press.

———. 2000. *Republics of Reality, 1975–1995*. Los Angeles: Sun and Moon Press.

———. 2001. *With Strings*. Chicago: University of Chicago Press.

———. 2006. *Girly Man*. Chicago: University of Chicago Press.

———. 2011. *Attack of the Difficult Poems*. Chicago: University of Chicago Press.

———. 2013. *Recalculating*. Chicago: University of Chicago Press.

———. 2015. "I Love Speech! (or anyway, it's complicated.) *Parsing* at 39." http://jacket2 .org/commentary/parsing.

———. 2016. *Pitch of Poetry*. Chicago: University of Chicago Press.

Bernstein, Charles, and David Antin. 2002. *A Conversation with David Antin*. New York: Granary Books.

Bishop, John. 1986. *Joyce's Book of the Dark*. Madison: University of Wisconsin Press.

Blanchot, Maurice. 1943. *Faux pas*. Paris: Gallimard.

———. 1949. *La part de feu*. Paris: Gallimard.

———. 1950. *Thomas l'obscur. Paris: Gallimard.*

———. 1953. *Celui qui ne m'accompagnait pas*. Paris: Gallimard.

———. 1955. *L'espace littéraire*. Paris: Gallimard.

———. 1959. *Le livre à venir*. Paris: Gallimard.

———. 1969. *L'entretien infini*. Paris: Gallimard.

———. 1973. *Le pa au delà*. Paris: Gallimard.

———. 1980. *L'écriture du désastre*. Paris: Gallimard

———. 1981. *The Madness of the Day/La folie du jour*. Barrytown NY: Station Hill Press.

———. 1982. *The Space of Literature*. Translated by Ann Smock. Lincoln: University of Nebraska Press.

———. 1986. *The Writing of the Disaster*. Translated b y Ann Smock. Lincoln: University of Nebraska Press.

———. 1988. *Thomas the Obscure*. Translated by Robert Lamberton. Barrytown, NY: Station Hill.

———. 1992. *The Step/Not Beyond*. Translated by Lycette Nelson. Albany: SUNY Press.

———. 1993a. *The Infinite Conversation*. Translated by Susan Hanson. Minneapolis: University of Minnesota Press.

———. 1993b. *The One Who Was Standing Apart from Me*. Translated by Lydia Davis. Barrytown NY: Station Hill Press.

———. 1995. *The Work of Fire*. Translated by Charlotte Mandell. Stanford: Stanford University Press.

———. 1997. *Awaiting Oblivion*. Translated by John Gregg. Lincoln: University of Nebraska Press.

———. 2001. *Faux Pas*. Translated by Charlotte Mandell. Stanford: Stanford University Press.

———. 2003. *The Book to Come*. Translated by Charlotte Mandell. Stanford: Stanford University Press.

Berryman, Sylvia. 2016. "Leucippus." Stanford Encyclopedia of Philosophy. Edited by Edward N. Zalta. https://plato.stanford.edu/archives/win2016/entries/leucippus/.

Boheemen, Christine Van. 1999. *Joyce, Derrida, Lacan, and the Trauma of* History: *Reading, Narrative, and Postcolonialism*. Cambridge: Cambridge University Press.

Bök, Christian. 2003. *Crystallography*. Toronto: Coach House Books.

Borg, Ruben. 2010. "Mirrored Disjunctions: On a Deleuzo-Joycean Theory of the Image." *Journal of Modern Literature* 33: 131–48.

Borowski, Tadeusz. 1976. "The Man with the Package." In *This Way for the Gas, Ladies and Gentlemen*, 147–51. London: Penguin Books.

Bradley, Richard. 2002. *Monuments and Landscape in Atlantic Europe: Perception and Society during the Neolithic and Early Bronze Age*. Edited by Chris Scarre. London: Routledge.

Brater, Enoch. 1994. *The Drama in the Text: Beckett's Late Fiction*. New York: Oxford University Press.

Bridgman, Richard. 1970. *Gertrude Stein in Pieces*. New York: Oxford University Press.

Brivic, Shelly. 2008. *Joyce through Lacan and Žižek: Explorations*. New York: Palgrave MacMillan.

Brooker, M. Keith. 1997. *Joyce, Bakhtin, and Literary Tradition: Toward a Comparative Cultural Poetics*. Ann Arbor: University of Michigan Press.

Brown, Jane. 2009. "Romanticism and Classicism." In *Cambridge Companion to German Romanticism*, edited by Nicholas Saul, 119–31. Cambridge: Cambridge University Press.

Brown, Marshall. 1979. *The Shape of German Romanticism*. Ithaca, NY: Cornell University Press.

Bruns, Gerald L. 1969. "The Storyteller and the Problem of Language in Samuel Beckett's Fiction." *Modern Language Quarterly* 10.2: 265–81.

———. 1971. "Samuel Beckett's *How It Is*." *James Joyce Quarterly* 8.4: 318–31.

———. 1974. *Modern Poetry and the Idea of Language: A Critical and Historical Study*. New Haven, CT: Yale University Press.

———. 1981. "A Short Defense of Plagiary." *Review of Contemporary Literature* 1.1: 96–103.

———. 1997. *Maurice Blanchot: The Refusal of Philosophy*. Baltimore: Johns Hopkins University Press.

———. 1999. *Tragic Thoughts at the End of Philosophy: Language, Literature, and Ethical Theory*. Evanston, IL: Northwestern University Press.

———. 2005. *The Material of Poetry: Sketches for a Philosophical Poetics*. Athens: University of Georgia Press.

———. 2006. *On the Anarchy of Poetry and Philosophy: A Guide for the Unruly.* New York: Fordham University Press.

Cage, John. 1961. *Silence.* Middletown, CT: Wesleyan University Press.

———. 1981. *Empty Words: Writings, '73–'78.* Middletown, CT: Wesleyan University Press.

———. 1983. *X: Writings, '79–'82.* Middletown, CT: Wesleyan University Press.

Campbell, Joseph, and Henry Morton Robinson. 1944. *A Skeleton Key to "Finnegans Wake."* New York: Harcourt Brace.

Campos, Augusto de. 1967. "uma vez." In *An Anthology of Concrete Poetry,* edited by Emmett Williams, n.p. New York: Something Else Press

Campos, Haroldo de. 1967. "Si." In *An Anthology of Concrete Poetry,* edited by Emmett Williams, n.p. New York: Something Else Press.

———. 1977. "Sanscreed Latinized: The *Wake* in Brazil and Hispanic America." *Triquarterly* 38: 48–60.

———. 1984. *Galaxias, 1963–1976.* São Paulo: ED Ex Libris.

———. 2007. *Novas: Selected Writings.* Translated by Suzanne Jill Levine and Jon Tolman. Evanston, IL: Northwestern University Press.

Canetti, Elias. 1994. *The Agony of the Flies.* Translated by H. G. Broch de Rothermann. New York: Farrar, Straus, and Cudahy.

Cavell, Stanley. 1969. *Must We Mean What We Say? A Book of Essays.* Cambridge: Cambridge University Press.

———. 1979. *The Claim of Reason: Wittgenstein, Skepticism, Morality, and Tragedy.* London: Cambridge University Press.

Celan, Paul. 1983. *Gesammelte Werke.* Vols. 1–3. Frankfurt am Main: Suhrkamp.

———. 1986. *Last Poems: A Bilingual Edition.* Translated by Katherine Washburn and Margret Guillemin. San Francisco: North Point Press.

Cooke, Jennifer. 2007. "Warring Inscriptions: J. H. Prynne's *To Pollen.*" www.intercapil laryspace.org/2007/04/warring-inscriptions-j-h-prynnes-to.html.

Crispi, Luca, and Slote, Sam. 2007. *How Joyce Wrote "Finnegans Wake": A Chapter by Chapter Guide.* Madison: University of Wisconsin Press.

Critchley, Simon. 2004. *Very Little, Almost Nothing: Death, Philosophy, Literature.* 2nd ed. London: Routledge Press.

———. 2007. *On Humour.* London: Routledge Press.

Culler, Jonathan. 1975. *Structuralist Poetics: Structuralism, Linguistics, and the Study of Literature.* Ithaca, NY: Cornell University Press.

cummings, e. e. 1998. *No Thanks.* Edited by George James Firmage. New York: Liveright Press.

DeKoven, Marianne. 1983. *A Different Language: Gertrude Stein's Experimental Writing.* Madison: University of Wisconsin Press.

Deleuze, Gilles. 1990. *The Logic of Sense.* Translated by Mark Lester. New York: Columbia University Press.

Deleuze, Gilles, and Félix Guattari. 1983. *Anti-Oedipus: Capitalism and Schizophrenia.* Translated by Robert Hurley, Mark Seem, Helen R. Lane. Minneapolis: University of Minnesota Press.

———. 1987. *A Thousand Plateaus: Capitalism and Schizophrenia.* Translated by Brian Massumi. Minneapolis: University of Minnesota Press.

Derrida, Jacques. 1984. "Two Words for Joyce." In Attridge and Ferrer, *Post-structuralist Joyce,* 144–59.

———. 1986. *Glas.* Translated by John P. Leavey Jr. and Richard Rand. University of Nebraska Press.

———. 1989. *Edmund Husserl's "Origin of Geometry: An Introduction."* Translated by John P. Leavey. Evanston, IL: Northwestern University Press.

Dobson, Kit. 2013. *Please, No More Poetry: The Poetry of derek beaulieu.* Waterloo, ON: Wilfrid Laurier University Press.

Dresher, Olivia, ed. 2006. *In Pieces: An Anthology of Fragmentary Writing.* Seattle: Impassio Press.

Drucker, Johanna. 1984. "Letterpress Language: Typography as a Medium for the Visual Representation of Language." *Leonardo* 17.1: 8–16.

———. 1994. *The Visible Word: Typography and Modern Art, 1909–1923.* Chicago: University of Chicago Press.

———. 2013a. *Stochastic Poetics.* Los Angeles: Druckwerk Facsimile Edition.

———. 2013b. *What Is? Nine Epistemological Essays.* Berkeley: Cuneiform Press.

Dworkin, Craig. 2013. *No Medium.* Cambridge, MA: MIT Press.

Dydo, Ulla E. 2003. *Gertrude Stein: The Language That Rises: 1923–1934.* Evanston, IL: Northwestern University Press.

Eco, Umberto. 1985. "The Semiotics of Metaphor." In *Semiotics: An Introductory Anthology,* edited by Robert Innis, 239–55. Bloomington: Indiana University Press.

Eliot, T. S. 1952. *Complete Poetry and Plays: 1909–1950.* New York: Harcourt Press.

Eng, Michael. 2012. "The Metaphysical Mouth and the Asylum of the Everyday: Charles Bernstein and Continental Philosophy of Language." In Allegrezza, *Salt Companion,* 35–54.

Epstein, Edmund. 2009. *A Guide through "Finnegans Wake."* Tallahassee: University of Florida Press.

Fairbanks, Arthur, ed. and trans. 1898. "Parmenides." In *The First Philosophers of Greece; An Edition and Translation of the Remaining Fragments of the Pre-Sokratic Philosophers, Together with a Translation of the More Important Accounts of Their Opinions Contained in the Early Epitomes of Their Works,* 104. New York: Scribner's Publishing.

Feuvre, Lisa le. 2010. *Failure.* Cambridge, MA: MIT Press.

Finch, Peter. 1972. *Typewriter Poems.* New York: Something Else Press.

Finney, Brian. 1987. "*Still to Worstward Ho*: Beckett's Prose Fiction Since *The Lost Ones.*" In *Beckett's Later Fiction and Drama,* edited by James Acheson and Kateryna Arthur, 65–79. London: Macmillan.

Flaubert, Gustave. 1953. *Selected Letters of Gustave Flaubert*. Edited by Francis Steegmuller. New York: Vintage Books.

Fort, Jeff. 2014. *The Imperative to Write: Destitution of the Sublime in Kafka, Blanchot, and Beckett*. New York: Fordham University Press.

Foucault, Michel. 1994. *Ethics, Subjectivity, and Truth*. Edited by Paul Rabinow. New York: New Press.

Frank, Joseph. 1945. "Spatial Form in Modern Literature." *Sewanee Review* 50.4: 643–53.

Frank, Manfred. 2003. *The Philosophical Foundations of Early German Romanticism*. Translated by Elizabeth Millan-Zaibert. Albany: SUNY Press.

Fredman, Stephen. 1990. *Poet's Prose: The Crisis in American Verse*. 2nd. ed. Cambridge: Cambridge University Press.

Friedrich, Hugo. 1956. *Die Struktur der modernen Lyric von Baudelaire bis zur Gegenwart*. Hamburg: Rowohit.

Gallego, Carlos. 2012. "From a Philosophy of Poetry to Poetry as Philosophy: The Dialectical Poetics of Charles Bernstein." In Allegrezza, *Salt Companion*, 208–33.

Gasché, Rodolphe. 2011. "The Imperative of Transparency: Maurice Blanchot's *the one who was standing apart from me*." In *The Stelliferous Fold: Toward a Virtual Law of Literature's Self-Formation*, 319–56. New York: Fordham University Press.

Gass, William H. 1971. "Gertrude Stein: Her Escape from Protective Language." In *Fiction and the Figures of Life*, 79–96. Boston: Nonpareil Books.

Glazier, Loss Paqueño. 2001. *Digital Poetics: The Making of E-Poetry*. Tuscaloosa: University of Alabama Press.

Gleick, James. 1987. *Chaos: Making a New Science*. New York: Viking Press.

Gordon, John. 1986. *"Finnegans Wake": A Plot Summary*. Syracuse, NY: Syracuse University Press.

Gregg, John. 1994. *Maurice Blanchot: The Literature of Transgression*. Princeton, NJ: Princeton University Press.

Gross, John. 1994. *The Oxford Book of Comic Verse*. Oxford: Oxford University Press.

Habermas, Jürgen. 1990. *The Philosophical Discourse of Modernity*. Translated by Frederick Lawrence. Cambridge, MA: MIT Press.

Hart, Clive. 1962. *Structure and Motif in "Finnegans Wake."* Evanston, IL: Northwestern University Press.

Hartman, Geoffrey. 1981. *Saving the Text: Literature/Derrida/Philosophy*. Baltimore: Johns Hopkins University Press.

Harrison, Charles, and Paul Wood. 1993. *Art in Theory, 1900–1990: An Anthology of Changing Ideas*. Oxford: Blackwell Publishers.

Hayman, David. 1990. *The "Wake" in Transit*. Ithaca, NY: Cornell University Press.

Heath, Stephen. 1984. "Ambiviolences: Notes for Reading Joyce." In Attridge and Ferrer, *Post-structuralist Joyce*, 31–68

Heidegger, Martin. 1971a. *Language, Poetry, Thought*. Translated by Richard Hofstadter. New York: Harper and Row.

————. 1971b. *On the Way to Language.* Translated by Peter Hertz. New York: Harper and Row.

Hejinian, Lyn. 2001. *The Language of Inquiry.* Berkeley: University of California Press.

Hill, Craig, and Nico Vassilakis. 2012. *The Last VISPO Anthology: Visual Poetry, 1998– 2002.* Salt Lake: Fantagraphics Books.

Hill, Leslie. 2012. *Maurice Blanchot and Fragmentary Writing: A Change of Epoch.* London: Contiuum.

Hoagland, Tony. 2006. "Fragment, Juxtaposition, and Completeness." *Cortland Review* 33. www.cortlandreview.com/issue 33/hoagland_e.html.

Hölderlin, Friedrich. 1969. *Hölderlin Werke und Briefe.* Vol. 1. Edited by Friedrich Beißner and Jochen Schmidt. Berlin: Insel Verlag.

————. 1984. *Hymns and Fragments.* Translated by Richard Sieburth. Princeton, NJ: Princeton University Press.

————. 2009. *Essays and Letters.* Translated by Jeremy Adler and Charles Louth. London: Penguin Books.

Holland, Michael. 2010. "Space and Beyond: *L'attente, l'oubli.*" In *Clandestine Encounters: Philosophy in the Narratives of Maurice Blanchot,* edited by Kevin Hart, 263–81. Notre Dame, IN: University of Notre Dame Press.

Horne, Haynes. 1997. "The Early German Romantic Fragment and Incompleteness." In Schulte-Sasse, *Theory as Practice,* 289–313.

Houlgate, Stephen, ed. 2007. *Hegel and the Arts.* Evanston, IL: Northwestern University Press.

Huang, J. P. 2003. "Giant Enhancement of Optical Nonlinearity in Mixtures of Graded Particles with Dialectric Anistrophy." *European Physical Journal* 36.4: 475–84.

Jameson, Fredric. 1984. "Postmodernism: Or, the Cultural Logic of Late Capitalism." *New Left Review* 146: 53–92.

Jarry, Alfred. 2001. *Adventures in 'Pataphysics.* Edited by Alastair Brotchie and Paul Edwards. London: Atlas Press.

Jarvis, Simon. 2003. "The Incommunicable Silhouette." *Jacket* 24, (November). http:// jacketmagazine.com/24/jarvis.html.

Jenkins, Linda Jones. 1997. "'Ce tourment qui est un rire': Maurice Blanchot with Samuel Beckett." *Romanic Review* 88.1: 1–17.

Johns, Gregory. 2010. *In the Dim Void: Samuel Beckett's Late Trilogy.* 4th ed. Maidstone, UK: Crescent Moon Publishing.

Joyce, James. 1958. *Finnegans Wake.* New York: Viking Press.

————. 1966. *A Portrait of the Artist as a Young Man.* New York: Viking Press.

————. 1986. *Ulysses.* Edited by Hans Walter Gabler. New York: Random House.

————. 1996. *Dubliners: Text and Criticism.* Edited by Robert Scholes and A. Walton Litz. London: Penguin Books..

Kac, Eduardo. 2007. *New Media Poetry: An International Anthology.* Bristol, UK: Intellect Press.

Kafka, Franz. 1949. *Diaries: 1910–1923*. Edited by Max Brod. Translated by Joseph Kresh. New York: Schocken Books.

Keats, John. 1959. *Selected Letters and Poems*. Edited by Douglas Bush. New York: Houghton Mifflin.

Kenner, Hugh. 1956. *Dublin's Joyce*. Boston: Beacon Hill.

———. 1987. *The Mechanic Muse*. New York: Oxford University Press.

Kenner, Hugh, and Charles Hartman. 1984. *Sentences*. Los Angeles: Sun and Moon Press.

Kershner, R. B. 1990. *Joyce, Bakhtin, and Popular Culture*. Chapel Hill: University of North Carolina Press.

Kierkegaard, Sóren. 1989. *The Concept of Irony: With Continual Reference to Socrates*. Translated by Howard V. Hong and Edna H. Hong. Princeton, NJ: Princeton University Press.

Kristeva, Julia. 1983. "Within the Microcosm of the 'Talking Cure.'" In *Interpreting Lacan*, edited by Joseph Smith and William Kerrigan, 38–49. New Haven, CT: Yale University Press.

Lacan, Jacques. 1972. *Encore: Le seminaire, livre xx*. Paris: Seuil.

———. 1977a. *Écrits: A Selection*. Translated by Alan Sheridan. New York: W. W. Norton.

———. 1977b. *Four Fundamental Concepts of Psychoanalysis*. Translated by Alan Sheridan. New York: W. W. Norton.

LaCapra, Dominick. 1983. *Rethinking History: Texts, Contexts, Language*. Ithaca, NY: Cornell University Press.

Lacoue-Labarthe, Philippe, and Jean-Luc Nancy. 1988. *The Literary Absolute: The Theory of Literature in German Romanticism*. Translated by Philip Barnard and Cheryl Lester. Albany: SUNY Press.

Lagapa, Jason. 2012. "To Think Figuratively, Tropically: Charles Bernstein's Post–9/11 Grammar and the Pragmatist Lessons in the Age of Baudrillard." In Allegrezza, *Salt Companion*, 172–91.

Langbaum, Robert. 1963. *The Poetry of Experience: The Dramatic Monologue in Modern Literary Tradition*. New York: W. W. Norton.

Lautman, Albert. 1938. *Les schemas de structure*. Paris: Hermann.

Lear, Edward. 1951. *The Complete Nonsense of Edward Lear*. Edited by Holbrook Jackson. London: Dover Books.

Lecercle, Jean-Jacques. 1985. *Philosophy through the Looking-Glass: Language, Nonsense, Desire*. LaSalle, IL: Open Court Press.

Lehman, David. 1999. *The Last Avant-Garde: The Making of the New York School of Poets*. New York: Anchor Books.

Leonard, Garry. 1991. "Joyce and Lacan: 'The Woman' as Symptom of 'Masculinity' in 'The Dead.'" *James Joyce Quarterly* 28: 451–72.

Levinas, Emmanuel. 1960. *Totality and Infinity*. Translated by Alphonso Lingis. Pittsburgh: Duquesne University Press.

———. 1987. *Collected Philosophical Papers.* Translated by Alphonso Lingis. The Hague: Nijhoff.

———. 1996. "The Servant and Her Master." In *Proper Names.* Translated by Michael B. Smith, 140–49. Stanford, CA: Stanford University Press.

Lewis, D. B. Wyndham, and Charles Lee. 2003. *The Stuffed Owl: An Anthology of Bad Verse.* New York: New York Review Books.

Locatelli, Carla. 1990. *Unwording the Word: Samuel Beckett's Prose Fiction after the Nobel Prize.* Philadelphia: University of Pennsylvania Press.

Lyotard, Jean-François. 1988. *The Differend.* Translated by Georges Van Den Abbeele. Minneapolis: University of Minnesota Press.

Mack, Anne, J. J. Rome, and Georg Mannejc. 1991. "Private Enigmas and Critical Functions, with Particular Reference to the Writings of Charles Bernstein." *New Literary History* 22.2: 441–64.

Mahon, Peter. 2007. *Imagining Joyce and Derrida: "Finnegans Wake" and "Glas."* Toronto: University of Toronto Press.

Mallarmé, Stéphane. 1956. *Mallarmé: Selected Poems, Essays, and Letters.* Translated by Bradford Cook. Baltimore: Johns Hopkins University Press.

———. 1965a. *Correspondance.* Edited by Henri Mondor. Paris: Pleiade.

———. 1965b. *Mallarmé.* Edited by Anthony Hartley. Baltimore: Penguin Books.

———. 1982. *Selected Poetry and Prose.* Edited by Mary Ann Caws. New York: New Directions.

———. 1992. *Œuvres de Mallarmé.* Edited by Yves-Alain Favre. Paris: Bordas.

Merleau-Ponty, Maurice. 1962. *The Phenomenology of Perception.* Translated by Colin Smith. London: Routledge Publishers.

———. 1964. *The Primacy of Perception and Other Essays on Phenomenological Psychology, the Philosophy of Art, History, and Politics.* Edited by James Edie. Translated by Carleton Dallery. Evanston, IL: Northwestern University Press.

———. 1968. *The Visible and the Invisible.* Edited by Claude Lefort. Translated by Alphonso Lingis. Evanston, IL: Northwestern University Press.

Michel, Andreas, and Assenka Oksiloff. 1997. "Romantic Crossovers: Philosophy as Art and Art as Philosophy." In Schulte-Sasse, *Theory as Practice,* 157–79.

Middleton, Peter. 1997. "Not Nearly Too Much Prynne." *Cambridge Quarterly* 26.4: 344–53.

———. 2004. "Poetry after 1970." In *Cambridge History of Twentieth-Century Literature,* edited by Laura Marcus and Peter Nicholls, 768–86. Cambridge: Cambridge University Press.

———. 2009. "Strips, Scientific Language in Poetry." *Textual Practice* 23: 947–58.

Miller, Nicholas A. 1993. "Beyond Recognition: Reading the Unconscious in the 'Ithaca' Episode of *Ulysses.*" *James Joyce Quarterly* 30: 209–18.

Misra, Durga. 2011. "Evolution of Dialectric Science and Technology for Nanoelectronics." *Interface* 20.4: 27–38.

Mittman, Elizabeth, and Mary R Strand. 1997. "Introductory Essay: Representing the Self and Other in Early German Romanticism." In Schulte-Sasse, *Theory as Practice*, 47–71.

Morris, Adelaide, and Thomas Swiss. 2006. *New Media Poetics: Contexts, Technotexts, and Theories.* Cambridge, MA: MIT Press.

Nordon, Kate Van. 1998. "On the Side of Poetry and Chaos: Mallarméan *Hasard* and Twentieth-Century Music." In *Meetings with Mallarmé in Contemporary French Culture*, edited by Michael Temple, 170–83. Exeter, UK: University of Exeter Press.

Norman, Judith. 2007. "Hegel and German Romanticism." In Houlgate, *Hegel and the Arts*, 310–36.

Norris, Margot. 1974. "The Language of Dream in *Finnegans Wake*." *Literature and Psychoanalysis* 24: 4–11.

———. 1976. *The De-Centered Universe of "Finnegans Wake."* Baltimore: Johns Hopkins University Press.

Nygaard, Loisa C. 1988. "Time in Schlegel's *Lucinde*." *Colloquia Germania* 13.4: 334–49.

O'Hara, Frank. 1995. *The Collected Poems of Frank O'Hara.* Edited by Donald Allen. Berkeley: University of California Press.

Parsegian, V. Adrian. 2006. *Van der Waals Forces: A Handbook for Biologists, Chemists, Engineers, and Physicists.* Cambridge: Cambridge University Press.

Perloff, Marjorie. 1981. *The Poetics of Indeterminacy.* Princeton, NJ: Princeton University Press.

———. 1985. *The Dance of the Intellect: Studies in the Poetry of the Pound Tradition.* Cambridge: Cambridge University Press.

———. 1986. *The Futurist Moment: Avant-Garde, Avant-Guerre, and the Language of Rupture.* Chicago: University of Chicago Press.

———. 1996. *Wittgenstein's Ladder: Poetic Language and the Strangeness of the Ordinary.* Chicago: University of Chicago Press.

———. 2004. *Differentials: Poetry, Poetics, Pedagogy.* Tuscaloosa: University of Alabama Press.

———. 2010. *Unoriginal Genius: Poetry by Other Means in the New Century.* Chicago: University of Chicago Press.

Peterson, Tim. 2012. "Either You're with Us and against Us: Charles Bernstein's *Girly Man*, 9/11, and the Brechtian Figure of the Reader." In Allegrezza, *Salt Companion*: 11–29.

Pietrzak, Wit. 2012. *Levity of Design: Man and Modernity in the Poetry of J. H. Prynne.* Newcastle upon Tyne, UK: Cambridge Scholars Publishing.

Pope, Alexander. 1963. *The Collected Poems of Alexander Pope.* Edited by John Butt. New Haven, CT: Yale University Press.

———. 2009. *The Art of Sinking in Poetry.* London: Oneworld Classics.

Prelutsky, Jack. 1940. "Last Night I Dreamed of Chickens." www.poets.org/poetsorg/poem/last-night-i-dreamed-chickens.

Prynne, Jeremy. 1962. "Resistance and Difficulty." *Prospect* 5: 25–41.

———. 2005. *Poems*. 2nd ed. Newcastle upon Tyne, UK: Bloodaxe Books.

———. 2011. *Kazoo Dreamboats; or, On What There Is*. Cambridge: Cambridge University Press.

———. 2016. "The Art of Poetry No 101" (interview). *Paris Review* 218: 174–207.

Quartermain, Peter. 1992. *Disjunctive Poetics: From Gertrude Stein and Louis Zukofsky to Susan Howe*. Cambridge: Cambridge University Press.

Rabaté, Jean-Michel. 1984. "Lapus ex machina." In Attridge and Ferrer, *Post-structuralist Joyce*, 79–102.

Raworth, Tom. 2003. *Collected Poems*. Manchester, UK: Carcanet.

Retallack, Joan. 1998. *How to Do Things with Words*. Los Angeles: Sun and Moon Press.

Ricoeur, Paul. 1970. *Freud and Philosophy: An Essay on Interpretation*. Translated by Denis Savage. New Haven, CT: Yale University Press.

———. 1977. *The Rule of Metaphor*. Translated by Robert Czerny. Toronto: University of Toronto Press.

Riddel, Alan. 1972. "Hologrammer." *Typewriter Poems*. Edited by Peter Finch. New York: Something Else Press.

Rimbaud, Arthur. 1962. *Collected Poems*. Edited by Oliver Bernard. London: Penguin Books.

Rorty, Amélie Oksenberg. 1988. "The Deceptive Self: Liars, Layers, and Lairs." In *Perspectives on Self-Deception*, edited by Brian P. McLaughlin and Amélie Oksenberg Rorty, 25. Berkeley: University of California Press.

Rothenberg, Jerome. 1974. *Revolution of the Word: New Gatherings of American Avant-Garde Poetry, 1914–1945*. Boston: Exact Change Press.

Roy, Ayon. 2009. "Hegel contra Schlegel; Kierkegaard contra de Man." *PMLA* 124.1: 107–26.

Savardi, Ugo, and Bianchi, Ivana. 2005. "Looking at Yourself in the Mirror: Structures of Perceptual Opposition." *Gestalt Theory* 27: 204–20.

Schlegel, Friedrich. 1991. *Philosophical Fragments*. Translated by Peter Firchow. Minneapolis: University of Minnesota Press.

———. 2013. *Athanäneums-Fragmente und andere Schriften*. Edited by Michael Holzinger. Berlin: Berliner Ausgabe.

Schotter, James. 2010. "Verbovocovisuals: James Joyce and the Problem of Babel." *James Joyce Quarterly* 48.1: 89–101.

Schulte-Sasse, ed. 1997. *Theory as Practice: A Critical Anthology of Early German Romantic Writings*. Minneapolis: University of Minnesota Press.

Schuster, Joshua. 2011. "The Making of 'Tender Buttons': Steins Subjects, Objects, and the Illegible." *Jacket 2*, April 21. http://jacket2.org/article/making-tender-buttons.

Sellars, John. 2007. "Chronos and Aiön: Deleuze and the Stoic Theory of Time." *COLLAPSE III*, November: 177–205. www.urbanomic.com.

Sewell, Elizabeth. 1952. *The Field of Nonsense*. London: Chatto and Windus.

———. 1985. "Poetry and Madness, Connected or Not?—and the Case of Hölderlin. *Psychiatry and Literature* 4: 41–69.

Seyhan, Azade. 1992. *Representation and Its Discontents: The Critical Legacy of German Romanticism.* Berkeley: University of California Press.

Solt, Mary Ellen. 1968. *Concrete Poetry: A World View.* Bloomington: Indiana University Press.

Sood, Amit. 2010. *Train Your Brain, Engage Your Heart, Transform Your Life: A Course in Attention and Interpretation Theory.* Createspace Publishing Platform.www.createspace .com/.

Southey, Robert. 1848. *The Complete Poetical Works of Robert Southey.* New York: Appleton.

Stein, Gertrude. 1961. *The Autobiography of Alice B. Toklas.* New York: Vintage Books.

———. 1971. *Writings and Lectures, 1909–1945.* Edited by Patricia Meyerowitz. Middlesex, UK: Penguin Books.

———. 1972. *Selected Writings of Gertrude Stein.* Edited by Carl Van Vechten. New York: Vintage Books.

———. 1975. *How to Write.* Edited by Patricia Meyerowitz. New York: Dover Books.

———. 1993. *A Stein Reader.* Edited by Ulla E. Dydo. Evanston, IL: Northwestern University Press.

———. 1994. *Stanzas in Meditation.* Los Angeles: Sun and Moon Press.

———.2002. *Tender Buttons.* Los Angeles: Green Integer Press.

Stephens, Paul. 2012. "Beyond the Valley of the Sophist: Charles Bernstein, Irony, and Solidarity." In Allegrezza, *Salt Companion,* 140–68.

Stevens, Wallace. 1964. *The Collected Poems of Wallace Stevens.* New York: Alfred A. Knopf.

Stewart, Susan. 1983. "Shouts in the Street: Bakhtin's Anti-linguistics." *Critical Inquiry* 10.2: 270–84.

Temple, Michael, ed. 1998. *Meetings with Mallarmé in Contemporary French Culture.* Exeter, UK: University of Exeter Press.

Templeton, John Douglas. 2009. "Many Voices: *Singing.*" In *A Manner of Utterance: The Poetry of J. H. Prynne,* edited by Ian Brinton, 133–44. Exeter, UK: Shearsman Books.

Thurber, James. "There Is an Owl in My Room." *New Yorker,* November 17, 1934.

Thurston, Luke. 2010. *James Joyce and the Problem of Psychoanalysis.* Cambridge: Cambridge University Press.

Thurston, Nick. 2006. *The Remains of Literature.* New York: Information as Material.

Tindall, William York. 1959. *A Reader's Guide to "Finnegans Wake."* New York: Farrar, Straus, Cudahy.

Tipping, Richard. 1994. "When You're Feeling Kind of Bonkers." In Gross, *Oxford Book,* 473–74.

Tsushima, Michiko. 2003. *The Space of Vacillation: The Experience of Language in Beckett, Blanchot, and Heidegger.* Bern, Switzerland: Peter Lang.

Tullett, Barrie. 2014. *Typewriter Art: A Modern Anthology.* London: Laurence King Publishing.

Waldrop, Michael. 1992. *Complexity: The Emerging Science at the Edge of Order and Chaos.* New York: Simon and Schuster.

Wasserstrom, William. 1975. "The Sursymamericubealism of Gertrude Stein." *Twentieth-Century Literature* 21.1: 90–106.

Watt, Daniel. 2007. *Fragmentary Futures: Blanchot, Beckett, Coetzee.* Ashby-de-la-Zouch, UK: Inkerman Press.

Welch, Lew. 1996. *How I Read Gertrude Stein.* Edited by Paul Schaffer. San Francisco: Grey Fox Press.

Weller, Shane. 2003. "Samuel Beckett and the End(s) of Man: Writing at the Limits of Experience." Doctoral thesis, Florida State University.

———. 2007. "Beckett/Blanchot: Debts, Legacies, Affinities." In *Beckett's Literary Legacies,* edited by Matthew Feldman and Mark Nixon, 22–39. Newcastle, UK: Cambridge Scholars Publishing.

———. 2013. "Post World War Two Paris." In *Samuel Beckett in Context,* edited by Anthony Ullmann, 160–72. Cambridge: Cambridge University Press.

Wheale, Nigel. 2009. "Crosswording: Paths through Red D Gypsum." In *A Manner of Utterance: The Poetry of J. H. Prynne,* edited by Ian Brinton, 163–85. Exeter, UK: Shearsman Books.

Wieners, John. 1975. "Understood Disbelief in Paganism, Lies, and Heresy." In *Behind the State Capitol or Cincinnati Pike: Cinema decoupages; verses, abbreviated prose insights,* 2. Boston: Good Gay Poets.

———. 1986. *Selected Poems: 1958–1984.* Edited by Raymond Foye. Santa Barbara, CA: Black Sparrow Press, 1986.

Wilkinson, John. 1994. *Flung Clear: Poems in Six Books.* Brighton, UK: Parataxis Editions.

———. 2001. *Effigies against the Light.* Cambridge, UK: Salt Publishing.

———. 2004. *Schedule of Unrest: Selected Poems.* Norfolk, UK: Salt Publishing.

———. 2007. *The Lyric Touch: Essays on the Poetry of Excess.* Cambridge, UK: Salt Publishing.

———. 2015. *Courses Matter-Woven.* Cambridge: Equipage.

Williams, Emmett. 1967. *An Anthology of Concrete Poetry.* New York: Something Else Press.

Williams, William Carlos. 1970. *Imaginations.* New York: New Directions, 1970.

———. 1985. *Selected Poems.* New York: New Directions.

———. 1992. *Paterson.* New York: New Directions.

Willits, Curt G. 2003. "Samuel Beckett and the End(s) of Man: Writing at the Limits of Experience." PhD diss., Florida State University.

———. 2005. "The Blanchot/Beckett Correspondence: Situating the Writer/Writing at the Limen of Naught." *Colloquy: Text, Theory, Critique* 10: 257–68.

Wittgenstein, Ludwig. 1958. *Philosophical Investigations.* Translated by G. E. M. Anscombe. New York: MacMillan.

Wordsworth, William. 1965. *Selected Poems and Prefaces*. Edited by Jack Stillinger. Cambridge: Riverside Editions.

Yeats, William Butler. 1966. *The Player Queen: The Variorum Edition of the Plays of W. B. Yeats*. Edited by Russel K. Alspach. New York: Macmillan Publishers

———. 1983. *The Collected Poems of W. B. Yeats*. Edited by Richard J. Finneran. New York: Macmillan Publishers.

Zend, Robert. 2014. "Typescape #7." In *Typewriter Art: A Modern Anthology*, edited by Barrie Tullett, 76. London: Laurence King Publishing.

Ziarek, Ewa. 1996. *The Rhetoric of Failure: Deconstruction of Skepticism, Reinvention of Modernism*. Albany: SUNY Press.

Žižek, Slavoj. 1997. "From Joyce-the-Symptom to the Symptom of Power." *Lacanian Ink* 11: 12–15.

Index